ON THE EDGE
OUT OF THE BLUE

Henry Billings
Melissa Billings

Series Editor: Amy Collins
Executive Editor: Linda Kwil
Production Manager: Genevieve Kelley
Marketing Manager: Sean Klunder
Cover Design: Michael E. Kelly

**McGraw-Hill
Contemporary**

Send all inquiries to:
McGraw-Hill/Contemporary
130 East Randolph Street, Suite 400
Chicago, Illinois 60601

ISBN: 0-07-285196-1

Printed in the United States of America.

1 2 3 4 5 6 7 8 9 10 QPD 08 07 06 05 04 03

The **McGraw·Hill** Companies

CONTENTS

SAMPLE LESSON

To the Student

Strange things that cannot be explained happen to people every day. Unidentified flying objects, meteors, and sudden lightning strikes have scared and mystified people for hundreds of years. The stories in *On the Edge: Out of the Blue* go deep into the mysteries of true crime, the paranormal, and medical science. The British government is suspected of covering up a connection between humans and mad cow disease. A woman is kidnapped by bounty hunters. A mile-wide asteroid may hit the earth in 2028, causing catastrophic damage. The government denies a UFO crashed in the Berwyn Mountains—but many residents claim they saw it with their own eyes. Only you can determine the truth.

As you read the stories in this book, you will be developing your reading skills. The lessons will help you increase your reading speed while you improve your reading comprehension, critical thinking skills, and vocabulary. Many of the exercises are similar to questions you will see on state and national tests. Learning how to complete them will help you prepare for tests you will take in the future. Some of the exercises encourage you to write sentence or paragraph responses. As you write your opinions, you will learn to support them with specific examples from the stories you read.

You may not believe in UFOs. You may think the Hale-Bopp comet never had a strange object in its tail. You might see a clue scientists have missed to cure hantavirus. One thing is for certain: you won't be able to take your eyes off each page until you've read the book cover to cover.

How to Use This Book

ABOUT THE BOOK *On the Edge: Out of the Blue* has ten units, each of which contains two stories and a lesson. The stories are about true crime, unsolved mysteries, and ordinary people who do very bizarre things. Each story is followed by a page of reading comprehension exercises. These exercises will help you to better understand the article. At the end of each unit are exercises that help develop vocabulary and critical thinking skills. These exercises will assist your understanding of the similarities between the two stories and relate them to your own experiences.

THE SAMPLE LESSON The first lesson in the book is a sample that demonstrates how the units are organized. The sample lesson will show you how to complete the exercises. The correct answers to the questions are included.

WORKING THROUGH EACH UNIT Begin each unit by looking at the photograph. Before you begin reading, think about your reaction to the photo and predict what you think the article might be about. Then read the article.

Sometimes you or your teacher may want to time how long it takes you to read a story. You can write your time in the circle at the end of each story. Use the Words-per-Minute Table on page 120 to find your reading speed and record it on the Plotting Your Progress graph on page 121. As you read through the book, you will be able to watch your reading speed improve on the graph.

After you read the article and record your speed, begin the exercises. The comprehension section will test your understanding of what you have read. The vocabulary exercises will include words that were used in both stories. The critical thinking exercises will help you build analytical skills. Some of the exercises will ask you to write a paragraph giving your thoughts and opinions about the stories. Answers to all the exercises can be found in the *On the Edge Teacher's Guide.*

SAMPLE LESSON

SELECTION 1

The Green Light

Luis Delgado was not afraid of danger. After all, danger was part of his job. Luis was a 28-year-old police officer in Haines City, Florida. He expected to run into trouble once in a while. But he was not prepared for what took place on March 19, 1992. On that night, something happened that terrified him.

Luis was working the night shift. At 3:50 A.M., he was in his patrol car. He was driving on 30th Street, an unlighted road that ran past a grove of fruit trees. Suddenly Luis saw a light in his rear view mirror. It was bright green. It seemed to be coming down out of the sky. And it seemed to be following him.

A few seconds later, the inside of the patrol car was bathed in the strange green light. Luis saw a glowing object flying along on the right side of his car. He was going about 40 miles an hour. The object stayed right with him. Twice he slowed down a little and the object moved in front of him. But both times it quickly dropped back along his right side.

Luis was frightened. He radioed his dispatcher. The call went through at 3:52 A.M. Luis asked the dispatcher to send backup officers to help him. "Something is following the vehicle," Luis said.

Then the object moved in front of Luis' car for the third time. The green light was so bright that Luis had to squint to see. The object looked like some sort of spacecraft. It was about 15 feet wide and was flying about 10 feet off the ground.

The bright light made it hard to see. Luis pulled his car over to the side of the road. When he did so, the engine died. The car's lights went out, too. When Luis stopped, the Unidentified Flying Object— or UFO—also stopped. It hovered in the air about 20 feet away from him.

Luis didn't know what to do. He tried to call the dispatcher again, but the radio had gone dead. Luis stared at the glowing UFO ahead of him. He saw a three-foot dome in the center of it. The whole thing was an odd shade of green. The color seemed to "flow" over the object. Even in the quiet of the night, Luis could hear no sound coming from it.

Then a bright white light began to shine from the UFO directly into the car. Luis fought off a rising sense of panic. He got out of the car. Slowly he began backing away from the light. He pulled out his walkie-talkie and tried to call the dispatcher again. But the walkie-talkie wouldn't work, either.

Luis noticed that the air around him felt strangely cold. The temperature in the region that night was a mild 60 degrees. But Luis was shivering, and he could see his breath.

Then, without warning, the UFO started to move again. It flew away at a dizzying speed. Two or three seconds later, it was out of sight. Still terrified, Luis slowly made his way back to his patrol car. He managed to sit down in the driver's seat. But he kept the door open and one foot on the ground. That was how the backup officers found him when they arrived at 3:56 A.M. He was shaking and crying. He was so scared that at first he couldn't even speak.

By the time the other officers arrived, Luis' police radio was working again. The car engine and lights were working, too. There was no sign of any UFO. Still, the officers who saw Luis knew that something had happened. Said Sergeant H.L. Bartley, "I don't doubt he saw something strange out there that morning."

Others didn't doubt it, either. Later that morning, Luis was given a physical exam. He was also given a psychological exam. Doctors found nothing wrong with him. Luis had no injuries. He showed no sign of mental illness. There was nothing to suggest that he was losing touch with reality.

In time, he recovered from his fright. He continued to do his job as a police officer. But seven years after the event, he still believed that what he had seen was real. "It's still so vivid in my mind," he said. "It was the strangest experience of my life."

Dr. Mark Rodeghier reviewed Luis' case. Dr. Rodeghier had spent years studying UFOs. To him, Luis' account sounded believable. Rodeghier knew of more than 400 other cases in which a UFO had seemed to stalk someone driving a car. Often the UFO flashed a bright light into the vehicle. Often people felt a change in the temperature of the air. And often the UFO left suddenly at a very high speed.

Some people have theories about why Luis' radio stopped working. The UFO might have created a strange electrical field. Luis' engine might have died because of some weird magnetic pull. Or perhaps the fuel line was affected by the sudden drop in temperature.

Everyone is sorry that no tests were done at the time. No one tested the patrol car. And no one tested the ground near where Luis stopped. Those who believe Luis think tests would have shown he was telling the truth. Those who don't believe him think tests would have shown he was lying.

When you finish reading, subtract your start time from your end time. This is how long it took you to read the selection. Enter your reading time below.

If you have been timed while reading this article, enter your reading time below. Then turn to the Words-per-Minute Table on page 120 and look up your reading speed (words per minute). Enter your reading speed on the graph on page 121.

Reading Time: Selection 1

_____ : _____
MINUTES   SECONDS

Work through the exercises on this page.
If necessary, refer back to the story.

UNDERSTANDING IDEAS Circle the letter of the best answer.

1. **The backup officers arriving on the scene knew something was wrong with Luis Delgado because he**

   A was colder than usual

   (B) *was crying and shaking*

   C had turned an odd shade of green

   D had his car door open and one foot on the ground

2. **Which picture BEST describes what Luis Delgado saw?**

   1. flying saucer   **2.** space shuttle

   3. airplane   **4.** streetlight

   (F) *Picture 1*

   G Picture 2

   H Picture 3

   J Picture 4

3. **Dr. Rodeghier believed Luis' story because**

   A he was not physically injured

   B he was so scared when he was found

   C tests showed that Luis was mentally ill

   (D) *it matched other descriptions of UFO sightings*

4. **Based on the information in the article, the reader can conclude that UFOs are**

   (F) *still a mystery*

   G always green

   H extremely cold

   J magnetic fields

SUMMARIZE For each blank, choose the word that best completes the meaning of the paragraph.

mental	speak	green
experience	believes	cold

Luis Delgado had a very strange

_____*experience*_____. He saw a

_____*green*_____ object flying near his car.

The air became _____*cold*_____, and his

car and police radio would not work. When backup

officers found him, he was so scared he couldn't even

_____*speak*_____. He was given a physical

exam and a _____*mental*_____ exam, but

nothing was wrong with him. Seven years later, Luis

Delgado still _____*believes*_____ that what he

saw was real.

IF YOU WERE THERE Imagine that you were being followed by a UFO. What would you do? Write a brief paragraph explaining your actions. Be sure to include examples from the story to support your response.

Like Luis Delgado, I would quickly call the police.

I would also get in touch with someone like

Dr. Rodeghier who had studied UFOs. Hopefully that

would help me understand what had happened.

Read the next article and complete the exercises that follow.

Mystery in the Mountains

People had never seen anything like it before. On the evening of January 23, 1974, bright green lights appeared in the sky over Chester, England. Dozens of people saw them, but no one knew what they were. They weren't stars. They weren't airplanes. They didn't form a pattern. They just zigzagged across the sky. They seemed to be moving toward the Berwyn Mountains in northeastern Wales.

Two hours later, a very large object was spotted over the Berwyn Mountains. The object seemed to be falling toward the ground.

Anne Williams lived in the area. She saw the object coming down. "It was like an electric bulb in shape, with rough edges," she said. "The object fell behind the hills at the back of my bungalow."

Fourteen-year-old Huw Lloyd saw it, too. He was watching TV. Huw lived in the small Welsh village of Llandrillo. He looked out the window and saw the object flying across the sky. He noted that it had a blinking blue light.

A few minutes later, the object apparently hit one of the mountains. The crash came at 8:38 P.M.

"The earth shook," said Anne Williams.

The crash rattled homes and lit up the sky. It knocked glasses off kitchen counters. It caused shelves to fall down. The blast was felt in Chester—and even farther away. People who lived 60 miles from the mountains felt it. It measured 4.5 on the Richter scale. That made it as strong as a small earthquake.

Following the crash, people rushed outside. They saw blue lights floating over a mountain called Cader Bronwen. Some saw orange lights as well. At least one man reported a strange noise. It was a buzzing sound, he said. It reminded him of a swarm of bees.

Many people thought an airplane had crashed. They saw police cars rushing toward the mountain. "I was amazed at how quickly the police responded and how many people came here," Huw Lloyd said.

Pat Evans was a nurse who lived in the area. She got a call from the police. They wanted her to come to the mountain and help any survivors of the crash. Pat gathered a few supplies. Then she climbed into her car and drove toward Cader Bronwen. As she neared the crash site, she saw something amazing. There was a strange object on the mountainside. It looked like some kind of spaceship. But it didn't look as if it had crashed. Instead, it seemed "quite intact." It was round, very big, and it gave off an orange glow.

Suddenly, police officers hurried up to Pat. They told her to leave the mountain. She explained why she had come. Still, they told her to leave. They wouldn't answer any of her questions. They just wanted her to get out. Pat was scared, so she turned around and went home.

Soon dozens of army trucks rolled into the area. British soldiers blocked off the roads. No one was allowed in. Shepherds couldn't even get up the mountain to check on their sheep. The roadblock stayed in place for several days. Then the army trucks left. The army announced that it had found nothing. It said there was no evidence of a crash of any kind.

Many people thought the government was covering up the truth. Rumors began to swirl. One woman said she had seen alien bodies scattered on the ground. A man told a detailed story to reporter Nick Redfern. Redfern wrote about it in his book *Cosmic Crashes*. The man did not want his real name used. So Redfern picked a pseudonym. He called the man "James Prescott."

Prescott was one of the soldiers who went to Cader Bronwen on the night of the crash. He and four other soldiers saw two long boxes on the ground. They loaded the boxes into their truck. They took the boxes to an army laboratory. When the boxes were opened, Prescott saw two dead aliens inside.

"It was obvious that the creatures were not of this earth," Prescott told Redfern. The bodies were five or six feet tall. They were shaped like humans, but were much, much thinner. "They looked almost skeletal with a covering skin," Prescott said.

Was James Prescott telling the truth? What about Pat Evans? And what about all the people who saw lights and heard or felt a crash that night? Many people believe a UFO really did crash on Cader Bronwen. These people say there were so many witnesses that they couldn't all have been deluded. But others disagree.

One man who disagrees is Andy Roberts. In 2000, Roberts wrote an article called "Fire on the Mountain." He said that there were indeed lights in the sky that night. But the lights didn't come from a UFO. They were meteors. Astronomers in Britain did record several meteors that night. The shaking ground could have been caused by a small earthquake. And the eyewitnesses might simply have been confused. Roberts calls their stories "a tangle of belief and wishful thinking."

Roberts might be right, but there is one piece of evidence that is hard to explain. In 1980, an engineer named Arthur Adams went to the crash site. He wanted to look around. Adams found small pieces of green metal lodged in the rocks. He took these back to his laboratory. He found that they carried a weird electrical charge.

And so a sense of mystery still lingers in the Berwyn Mountains. People want to know what really happened there. Did an alien spacecraft crash on that lonely mountain? Or did people just let their imagination run away with them?

If you have been timed while reading this article, enter your reading time below. Then turn to the Words-per-Minute Table on page 120 and look up your reading speed (words per minute). Enter your reading speed on the graph on page 121.

Reading Time: Selection 2

_____ : _____
MINUTES   SECONDS

UNDERSTANDING IDEAS Circle the letter of the best answer.

| People in England saw bright green lights. | → | A very large object was spotted. | → | | → | Police cars rushed toward the mountain. |

1. Which statement below belongs in the empty box?

A Green lights zigzagged across the sky.

B No one was allowed to go up the mountain.

C Nurse Pat Evans was called to help survivors.

D There was a huge crash that shook the earth.

2. Which statement best summarizes the opinion of Andy Roberts?

F The army was trying to cover up the incident.

G An alien spacecraft crashed on the mountain.

H The lights in the sky were caused by meteors.

J The aliens were shaped like humans but thinner.

3. Which is the most convincing evidence that something unusual did crash into the Berwyn Mountains?

A Green metal that had a weird electrical charge was found at the site.

B Astronomers recorded several meteors that night.

C The government covered up the truth.

D The crash was as strong as a small earthquake.

4. Skeptics think the British army probably closed the mountain because

F there was nothing to see

G there had been a serious plane crash

H they wanted to keep the boxes with aliens inside for themselves

J they wanted to keep people from seeing what was there

SUMMARIZE For each blank, choose the word that best completes the meaning of the paragraph.

miles	spotted	lights
crashed	blocked	spacecraft

On January 23, 1974, people saw strange

_____ in the sky over

Chester, England. A few hours later, a large object

was _____ over the Berwyn

Mountains in Wales. At 8:38 P.M., the object apparently

_____ into the mountains. People

felt the impact _____ away, and

police cars rushed up the mountain. Soon after, the roads

were _____ off and no one was

allowed up the mountain. Many people believe an alien

_____ crashed that night.

IF YOU WERE THERE Write a brief paragraph explaining what you would do if you had seen and heard the crash in Wales. Be sure to include examples from the story to support your response.

_____

_____

_____

_____

_____

USE CONTEXT CLUES When you read, you may find a word whose meaning is unfamiliar to you. When that happens, you can look up the word's meaning in the dictionary. You can also find out what the word means by looking for context clues. These are words or sentences that come before or after the word. Context clues can be synonyms or antonyms of the unfamiliar word. They may also be an example or definition of the unfamiliar word.

Read each excerpt from the stories you just read. Circle the letter with the best meaning of the underlined word.

1. **The object looked like some sort of spacecraft. It was about 15 feet wide and was flying 10 feet off the ground. . . . It hovered in the air about 20 feet away from him.**

   A sank

   B burned

   C floated

   D rose

2. **The temperature in the region that night was a mild 60 degrees. But Luis was shivering, and he could see his breath.**

   F relaxing

   G gentle

   H freezing

   J harsh

3. **But seven years after the event, he still believed that what he saw was real. "It's still so vivid in my mind," he said.**

   A hazy

   B green

   C clear

   D forgotten

4. **But it didn't look like it had crashed. Instead, it seemed "quite intact."**

   F broken, shattered

   G motionless

   H loose

   J undamaged, complete

5. **The man did not want his real name used. So Redfern picked a pseudonym.**

   A false name

   B family name

   C middle name

   D real name

PUT WORDS INTO CONTEXT Complete the paragraph using the underlined words from the exercise on this page.

Many people claim that they have seen a UFO. Luis

Delgado says a spaceship _____

in the air, 20 feet from his patrol car. The temperature

that night was _____ , but the air

around the spaceship was very cold.

Residents of the Berwyn Mountains have also seen

strange things. People said they saw an alien spaceship

that was still _____ . Some

witnesses would only talk about what they had seen

using a _____ . Many people have

a _____ memory of what

happened that night.

ANTONYMS An antonym is a word that has the opposite meaning of another word. For example, *remember* is an antonym for the word *forget*.

Circle the letter of the word or phrase that means the OPPOSITE of the underlined word.

1. **On that night, something happened that <u>terrified</u> him.**

   A calmed

   B excited

   C scared

   D tricked

2. **It flew away at a <u>dazzling</u> speed.**

   F bright

   G fast

   H surprising

   J slow

3. **He noted that it had a <u>blinking</u> blue light.**

   A colored

   B shining

   C steady

   D swirling

4. **"They looked almost <u>skeletal</u> with a covering skin," Prescott said.**

   F tall

   G plump, muscular

   H thin

   J scary

5. **The shaking ground could have been <u>caused</u> by a small earthquake.**

   A noticed

   B prevented

   C started

   D worsened

ANTONYM ANALOGIES Analogies show similar patterns between words. Antonym analogies show patterns between words that have opposite meanings. For example, *large* is to *small* as *tall* is to *short*. For each blank, choose an underlined word from the exercise on this page to correctly complete the analogy.

1. *Stopped* is to *started* as *prevented* is to

   _____ .

2. *Dull* is to *brilliant* as *sluggish* is to

   _____ .

3. *Fearless* is to *afraid* as *calm* is to

   _____ .

4. *Fat* is to *skinny* as *fleshy* is to

   _____ .

5. *Constant* is to *flickering* as *steady* is to

   _____ .

ORGANIZE THE FACTS

ORGANIZE THE FACTS There are several different ways to organize your writing. In stories like the ones you just read, the sequence, or order, of the events is very important. In the chart below, fill in the next event(s) in the order that they happened.

"The Green Light"
1. On March 19, 1992, Luis Delgado was driving in his patrol car in Haines City, Florida.
2. He was being followed by a glowing object.
3. Luis radioed the dispatcher and asked for help.
4. The light was so bright, Luis had to stop the car.
5.

"Mystery in the Mountains"
1. On January 23, 1974, bright green lights were seen in the sky over Chester, England.
2.
3.
4.
5.

PUT DETAILS IN SEQUENCE

PUT DETAILS IN SEQUENCE Choose the best answer.

1. **When did the below happen? Where should it be in the sequence chart "The Green Light"?**

> When Luis sped up, the object sped up. When Luis slowed down, the object slowed down.

A before 1

B between 1 and 2

C between 2 and 3

D between 3 and 4

2. **In the chart "Mystery in the Mountains," where would you place the information about soldiers setting up a roadblock?**

F at the beginning of the list

G in the middle of the list

H toward the end of the list

J nowhere on the chart

DRAW CONCLUSIONS A conclusion is a judgment based on information you know. You draw a conclusion by thinking about what you've read and then seeing if you can make a judgment or general statement about it. Read this paragraph about UFOs. Then choose the best answer to each question.

[1] Many people who believe they have seen UFOs describe the same characteristics. [2] Often these people have felt a change in the temperature outside. [3] They usually see a bright light or many bright lights. [4] UFOs are said to have strange electrical fields or magnetic pulls. [5] Cars and radios sometimes stop working.

1. **Which conclusion can you draw based on the paragraph above?**
   A UFO sightings usually happen at night.
   B UFO sightings are often very similar.
   C UFO sightings always happen on holidays.
   D UFO sightings are never the same.

2. **Which sentence from the paragraph helps you conclude that UFOs might have lights?**
   F Sentence 1
   G Sentence 2
   H Sentence 3
   J Sentence 4

3. **Which sentence from the paragraph helps you conclude that UFOs sometimes cause machines to break down?**
   A Sentence 1
   B Sentence 2
   C Sentence 3
   D Sentence 5

JUDGE THE EVIDENCE When you make a conclusion, you must judge if the information presented is accurate or convincing. Choose the best answer.

1. **Which statement supports the conclusion that the British government was hiding what happened on the mountain?**
   A Rumors began to swirl.
   B The shaking ground could have been caused by a small earthquake.
   C Many people thought an airplane had crashed.
   D Adams found pieces of green metal carrying an electrical charge at the crash site.

2. **Which statement supports the conclusion that the lights in the sky were not from a UFO?**
   F Astronomers recorded several meteors that night.
   G There were indeed lights in the sky that night.
   H The eyewitnesses all claim to have seen the UFO.
   J Prescott saw two dead aliens inside the box.

YOUR OWN CONCLUSION Pretend that you are a police officer hearing a report of a UFO sighting. You must decide if it truly happened. State your conclusion and support it with examples from both stories.

_____

_____

_____

_____

SELECTION 1

The Strange Case of Thomas Root

It started out as a routine flight. Washington, D. C., lawyer Thomas Root climbed into his four-seat Cessna plane. He took off from National Airport at 6:33 A.M. on July 20, 1989. Root was a skilled pilot. He often flew to business meetings. This flight was meant to be a short one. He was going to Rocky Mount, North Carolina, just 156 miles away. This quick hop should have taken a little over an hour. But Thomas Root never made it to Rocky Mount.

At 8:30 A.M., Root was already 45 minutes late. At this point, he radioed that he was having chest pains. He said he was also having difficulty breathing. As the Federal Aviation Administration received his message, Root's plane crossed over the coast and headed out to sea. The Air Force sent a rescue plane out to follow him. Root did not respond to radio calls. So no one really knew what was wrong with him.

The rescue plane got close enough for its crew to see Root. He seemed to be sprawled out in the cockpit. Some members of the rescue team thought he looked unconscious. The Cessna, on automatic pilot, kept flying south at 10,000 feet. After four hours, the plane was 800 miles from Washington. Then it ran out of gas. It dropped from the sky. "We watched him spiral down from 10,000 feet. We were right on top of him," said Captain Alan Daniel, the pilot of the rescue plane.

Major Dave Yoak was the co-pilot of the rescue plane. He knew there was very little chance anyone could live through such a crash. Hitting the water from that height was like hitting a stone wall. "[The plane] dug in its left wing and then the cockpit hit," said Yoak. "When it came to a stop, the cockpit was under water. It was a violent crash."

Four medics parachuted into the sea. They thought they would be recovering a dead body. But instead, they got the shock of their lives. Root was still alive. And he was *swimming toward them!* The first medic to reach Root asked him how he was doing and what injuries he had. Root gave his name and said he had a pain in his stomach. He also said he was having trouble breathing. (Indeed, doctors later found that his ribs were fractured.) After the medics pulled Root into the rescue raft, they saw a wound in his stomach. They thought he had been cut by a piece of metal from the plane.

Later, at the hospital, doctors discovered the truth. Root hadn't been cut by a piece of metal. He had been shot! The bullet had entered his stomach. Then it had gone into his colon, left his body, and reentered by way of his left arm. The bullet had made three holes in his body. How could Root have survived the crash *and* three bullet wounds? People called it a "miracle."

The stomach wound suggested that Root had been shot at close range. There was a powder burn on his skin where the bullet had entered. Yet Root had been the only one in the plane. Had he tried to kill himself? Had the whole flight been just a show to make his death look like an accident?

Root said he didn't remember anything from the time he blacked out on the plane until he hit the water. He said he always carried a gun in the plane's glove compartment. He suggested it had gone off when the plane hit the water. Gun experts said that was almost impossible. Someone had to have pulled the trigger. But Root flatly denied that he had tried to kill himself.

Root was turning from miracle man into mystery man. Then police found out he was in debt. He owed his landlord $50,000. He owed $64,000 in back taxes. He had other troubles as well. His law clients complained that he hadn't kept his promises. And he had made some pretty shady business deals. One lawyer said of Root, "That man was Trouble with a capital T." On top of all this, the U. S. Customs Service was watching him as a possible drug smuggler.

Root recovered from his wounds. But he could not escape his other troubles. The drug charges were dropped. But in 1990, he was found guilty of fraud. The courts held that he had swindled his clients out of $5 million.

Root agreed to confess everything in return for a lighter sentence. Even so, he got fifteen years in prison. Thomas Root remained a mystery to the end. It was hard to imagine anyone being happy about spending that much time in prison. Yet Root was. He said the plea agreement was "so attractive to me that I could not refuse it."

If you have been timed while reading this article, enter your reading time below. Then turn to the Words-per-Minute Table on page 120 and look up your reading speed (words per minute). Enter your reading speed on the graph on page 121.

Reading Time: Selection 1

_____ : _____
MINUTES   SECONDS

UNDERSTANDING IDEAS Circle the letter of the best answer.

1. Which statement belongs in the empty box?

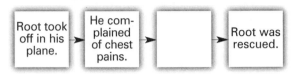

A Root was sentenced to prison.

B Root didn't remember anything.

C Root was late for a meeting.

D Root passed out and the plane crashed.

2. Which statement best summarizes why Root was called the miracle man?

F He was a very good pilot and lawyer.

G He was involved in shady business deals.

H He survived a plane crash and three bullet wounds.

J He was quickly rescued by medics.

3. Which is the most convincing evidence that Thomas Root might have shot himself?

A It is unlikely that the gun went off by itself.

B There was a powder burn on Root's stomach.

C Root always carried a gun on the plane.

D The bullet entered his stomach.

4. The jury probably found Thomas Root guilty because

F the gun could not have gone off by itself

G his plane crashed

H he had stolen money from his law clients

J all of the above

SUMMARIZE For each blank, choose the word that best completes the meaning of the paragraph.

radioed	rescue	commit
wounds	boarded	crashed

On July 20, 1989, Thomas Root

_____ his plane in Washington, D.C.

While in the air, he said he began having chest pains

and _____ for help. When the

_____ plane arrived, its crew

saw Root was passed out. Then Root's plane

_____ into the sea. Amazingly,

Root survived the crash and three bullet

_____. Later, police realized Root

may have been trying to _____

suicide.

IF YOU WERE THERE Write a brief paragraph explaining what you would do if you were one of Thomas Root's law clients. Would you believe his story? Be sure to include examples from the story to support your response.

_____

_____

_____

_____

_____

Loose Cannons on Board

Where is the worst place to be when someone goes berserk? How about being trapped in a plane high above the ground? You can't call the police. You can't dial 911. You can't get up and run away. All you can do is hope that the crew can somehow control the person until the plane lands. That isn't always easy.

It's really hard when *two* passengers go crazy. That happened on April 19, 2001. Cynthia and Crystal Mikula were on a United Airlines flight to China. The 22-year-old twins were models. They were going to China on business. During the in-flight movie, they both ordered several drinks. After the movie, they left their seats and headed for the restrooms. As they reached the rear of the plane, they began to shout. Cynthia screamed at her sister, "I've gotta get out of here. Let me off this airplane. I gotta smoke."

A flight attendant tried to calm her down. Cynthia hit the woman in the face, giving her a bloody nose. She then hit two other attendants and spat on a fourth. At last, the crew got out plastic handcuffs. They slapped these on Cynthia's wrists and ankles. At that point, her twin sister Crystal flew into a rage. She hit one crew member. Then she jumped on the back of another. She choked him and scratched his back. At last she, too, was brought under control.

All of this took place while the plane was over the Pacific Ocean. The pilot was alarmed. His crew was being attacked. So he turned the plane around and headed for the nearest airport. That was a thousand miles away, in Anchorage, Alaska. After the plane landed, the twins were arrested. They were charged with interfering with a flight crew. Under federal law, that is a felony.

Five months later, the twins were found guilty. The judge ordered Cynthia to pay $86,774.92. That was how much it had cost to divert the plane to Anchorage. The judge ordered her to do 231 hours of community service. That was one hour for every passenger on the jet. He also banned her from flying on any commercial plane for five years. Crystal got a lighter sentence. The judge fined her $500 for assault. He ordered her to do 231 hours of community service. And he banned her from flying for two years.

What happened with the twins is called air rage. It doesn't happen very often. But when it does, it can be very scary. On one plane, a mentally ill man broke into the cockpit of a plane and fought with the crew. He nearly caused the plane to crash. On another plane, a man went crazy when a crew member asked him to turn off his laptop. The man hit the crew member over the head with an in-flight telephone.

What sets these people off? Perhaps it is the crowded seats. Airlines pack as many seats as possible onto their planes. Some people can't stand being in such cramped quarters for a long time. Another reason might be the long lines at airports. These can put people in a foul mood even before take-off. But the biggest problem is alcohol. Passengers can buy all the drinks they want. In fact, in First Class, the drinks are free. Airlines have always made it easy for people to drink. They have felt that a drink or two helps nervous flyers relax. Also, airlines want passengers to be happy. They know that some people might turn ugly if they are *not* allowed to drink.

Most people who drink too much just doze off. But a few turn violent. Just ask Fiona Weir. Weir was a flight attendant with British Airtours. In October 1998, she was working on a flight from England to Spain. Even before take-off, she noticed that one of the passengers was drunk. Steven Handy was also abusive. Weir warned him not to smoke in the bathroom. Handy swore at her and demanded a drink. Weir wanted to have him removed from the plane. But her boss said no. Airtours was a charter company. It took people to vacation spots to have fun. It didn't want to upset anyone. So Weir was told to make the best of it. She was told to move Handy to the back of the plane, away from the other passengers.

All during the flight, Handy caused trouble. Then, just before the plane landed in Spain, he grabbed a vodka bottle. He smashed Weir over the head with it. Glass cut into Weir's face. Handy took the broken bottle and attacked Weir again. He raked the jagged glass over her back and legs as she lay on the floor. She needed eighteen stitches to close her wounds.

The Spanish police arrested Handy. He was given four years in prison for his actions. The British banned him from flying on any British airline for life. As for Fiona Weir, she would carry the scars from his attack forever.

If you have been timed while reading this article, enter your reading time below. Then turn to the Words-per-Minute Table on page 120 and look up your reading speed (words per minute). Enter your reading speed on the graph on page 121.

Reading Time: Selection 2

_____ : _____
MINUTES   SECONDS

UNDERSTANDING IDEAS Circle the letter of the best answer.

1. **Fiona Weir's injuries were a direct result of being**

   A arrested for threatening the flight crew

   B in a fight with a mentally ill man

   C attacked by a drunken passenger

   D involved in a plane crash

2. **Cynthia Mikula's actions on the plane were most likely caused by**

   F drinking too much

   G sitting still for too long

   H being unable to use a laptop

   J bad airplane food

3. **According to the article, air rage is often caused by**

   A long lines

   B crowded seats

   C too much alcohol

   D all of the above

4. **The reader can conclude that people who get air rage are**

   F extremely violent

   G always polite

   H satisfied with their seat assignment

   J flying to Alaska

SUMMARIZE For each blank, choose the word that best completes the meaning of the paragraph.

struck	plane	cramped
		attacked
charged	passengers	drink

Air rage happens when one or more

_____ lose control during a flight.

Often, flight attendants are _____.

They have been _____ with fists,

telephones, and even broken bottles. Sometimes the

people are frustrated by the _____

seats. Other times they have had too much to

_____. Passengers who attack other

people on a _____ can be

_____ with assault and interfering

with a flight crew.

IF YOU WERE THERE What would you do if you were on a flight with someone who had air rage? Write a brief paragraph explaining your actions. Be sure to include examples from the story to support your response.

_____

_____

_____

_____

_____

_____

USE CONTEXT CLUES When you read, you may find a word whose meaning is unfamiliar to you. When that happens, you can look up the word's meaning in the dictionary. You can also find out what the word means by looking for context clues. These are words or sentences that come before or after the word. Context clues can be synonyms or antonyms of the unfamiliar word. They may also be an example or definition of the unfamiliar word.

Read each excerpt from the stories you just read. Circle the letter with the best meaning of the underlined word.

1. **He seemed to be sprawled out in the cockpit. Some members of the rescue team thought he looked unconscious.**

   A passed out

   B in pain

   C comfortable

   D confused

2. **He also said he was having trouble breathing. (Indeed, doctors later found that his ribs were fractured.)**

   F hurting

   G sticky

   H broken

   J loose

3. **Root agreed to confess everything in return for a lighter sentence. Even so, he got fifteen years in prison.**

   A case load

   B drug charge

   C hospital bill

   D punishment

4. **The pilot was alarmed. His crew was being attacked. So he turned around and headed for the nearest airport.**

   F loud

   G afraid

   H confused

   J distracted

5. **After the plane landed, the twins were arrested. They were charged with interfering with a flight crew.**

   A preventing the work of

   B singing and dancing with

   C viciously attacking

   D helping politely

PUT WORDS INTO CONTEXT Complete the paragraph using the underlined words from the exercise on this page.

A passenger with air rage can make the flight crew

of an airplane quite _____. Flight

attendants have _____ bones trying to

subdue passengers. They have even been knocked

_____. Passengers who have air rage

attacks are charged with _____ with

a flight crew. The judge may _____ the

attacker to time in jail.

SYNONYMS A synonym is a word that has the same, or nearly the same, meaning as another word. For example, *happy* and *glad* are synonyms.

Circle the letter of the word that has almost the SAME meaning as the underlined word.

1. **Root did not respond to radio calls.**

   A overtake

   B exit

   C answer

   D surprise

2. **It was a violent crash.**

   F small and easy

   G graceful

   H powerful and rough

   J professional

3. **These can put people in a foul mood even before take-off.**

   A sleepy

   B cheerful

   C angry

   D calm

4. **At this point, twin sister Crystal went nuts.**

   F quiet

   G crazy

   H screaming

   J hungry

5. **He also banned her from flying on any commercial plane for five years.**

   A local

   B personal

   C large

   D public

SYNONYM ANALOGIES Analogies show relationships between words. Synonym analogies show patterns between words that have similar meanings. For example, *big* is to *large* as *little* is to *small*. For each blank, choose an underlined word from the exercise on this page to correctly complete the analogy.

1. *Call* is to *summon* as *reply* is to

   _____.

2. *Angry* is to *mad* as *insane* is to

   _____.

3. *Private* is to *personal* as *public* is to

   _____.

4. *Strength* is to *power* as *ferocious* is to

   _____.

ORGANIZE IDEAS The main ideas in a story are the larger, more general topics that are covered. The specific details are the facts that clarify or support the main ideas. Fill in the chart by using the items listed at the right. If the bulleted item is a main idea from the story, write it in the row marked "Main Idea." If the item is a detail that supports the main idea, write it in a row marked "Detail."

"The Strange Case of Thomas Root"
Main Idea:
Detail:
Detail:
Detail:
Detail:

"Loose Cannons on Board"
Main Idea:
Detail:
Detail:
Detail:
Detail:

- Air rage happens when people drink too much or get frustrated on airplanes.

- Root did not respond to radio calls.

- On one plane, a mentally ill man fought with the crew.

- Root said he didn't remember anything.

- Then the police found out he was in debt.

- A man went crazy when asked to turn off his laptop.

- Root agreed to confess everything in return for a lighter sentence.

- Cynthia hit the woman in the face, giving her a bloody nose.

- It is possible that Thomas Root's flight was a show to make his death look like an accident.

- All during the flight, Steven Handy caused trouble.

SUPPORT THE MAIN IDEA Write a paragraph about air rage. State the main idea in the first sentence. Then use details from both stories to support your main idea.

_____

_____

_____

_____

_____

_____

DRAW CONCLUSIONS A conclusion is a judgment based on information. The way you draw a conclusion is to think about what you've read and to see if you can make a judgment, or general statement, about it. Read this paragraph about air rage. Then choose the best answer to each question.

[1] Air rage can cause people to be extremely violent. [2] Often passengers or flight attendants are injured. [3] Angry passengers have hit, kicked, bit, and spit on people trying to hold them back. [4] Some people with air rage are simply tired of sitting still. [5] Other people are extremely drunk and violent.

1. **Which conclusion can you draw based on the paragraph above?**

    A Air rage is dangerous and should be taken seriously.

    B People with air rage are easy to control and calm down.

    C Air rage makes passengers want to sit very still.

    D A drink or two may help nervous passengers relax.

2. **Which sentence from the paragraph explains who may be a victim of air rage?**

    F Sentence 1

    G Sentence 2

    H Sentence 3

    J Sentence 4

3. **Which sentence from the paragraph helps you conclude that air rage can be caused by alcohol?**

    A Sentence 2

    B Sentence 3

    C Sentence 4

    D Sentence 5

JUDGE THE EVIDENCE When you make a conclusion, you must judge if the information presented is accurate or convincing. Choose the best answer.

1. **Which statement best supports the conclusion that Thomas Root's plane crash was an accident?**

    A Root owed back taxes.

    B He was in debt to his landlord.

    C The rescue team thought he looked unconscious.

    D Root flatly denied he was trying to kill himself.

2. **Which statement best supports the conclusion that Thomas Root was trying to commit suicide?**

    F Root had a lot of debt and was in trouble with the law.

    G He said he always carried a gun on the plane.

    H Root denied that he had tried to kill himself.

    J Root was turning from miracle man to mystery man.

YOUR OWN CONCLUSION Pretend that you are part of a jury that must decide whether Thomas Root staged his own death or not. State your conclusion and support it with examples from both stories.

_____

_____

_____

_____

_____

_____

Your Keys or Your Life

They strike out of nowhere. You could be stopped at a red light or parked in front of a convenience store when suddenly someone jumps into the seat beside you and orders you to get out. Or you might be getting into your car after doing a little shopping when someone knocks you down, grabs your keys, and drives off with your car.

You could even be in your own driveway when the attack occurs. That's what happened to a senior citizen in Toronto, Canada, in March 2001. He was standing next to his Mercedes SUV when two men approached. "Give me those keys!" shouted one.

"No way, buster," the elderly man responded.

The two young men knocked him to the ground, kicking him and trying to pry the keys out of his hand. The old man held the keys tight and did his best to fight back. At last, the two attackers fled without the keys.

The old man was lucky. In such cases, the police say, you should always surrender the keys. Your life is more important than your car. And if the carjacker also tries to rob you, you should just hand over the money. Only in extreme circumstances should you fight back.

Katoria Lee didn't want to fight when she was confronted by a carjacker in March of 2001, but she had no choice. Lee had just finished her night shift at an automobile plant in Hapeville, Georgia. It was almost 2:00 A.M. when she picked up her nine-year-old son, David, who had been staying at a cousin's house. As David slept in the back seat, Lee stopped her Ford Explorer at a 24-hour Wal-Mart to pick up a few things. The parking lot was well lighted, and Lee parked right in front of the entrance. She planned to dash in and out of the store, so she didn't bother to wake David.

When she emerged from the store, however, a young man appeared and pointed a gun at her. Lee tried to run back inside the store. The man fired three shots. One bullet hit Lee in the arm and another hit her in the back. She dropped the keys from her hand, thinking that was what the man wanted. Then Lee remembered David asleep in the car. "What else do you want?" she cried. "I gave you my keys. You want my purse? Could I at least get my son?"

Lee threw down her purse. The man grabbed the purse and the keys. He jumped into the Explorer and locked the doors, ignoring Lee's pleas to let her son go. Lee reacted the way most mothers would. Forgetting her own pain, she raced to the Explorer and began pounding on the side window to wake up her son. David awoke and unlocked the door. Lee ripped the door open and pulled him out as the thief drove off.

Lee was badly wounded. She thought she might even bleed to death. She called to three teenagers in a nearby car, but they paid no attention to her. Lee later discovered that they were with the young man who shot her.

Katoria Lee survived her ordeal, but said, "I'll never be the same." She underwent four operations and suffered from violent nightmares. For her, the only good news was that her attacker was caught and sentenced to fifteen years in prison. His three friends got sentences ranging from four to ten years.

In Denver, Colorado, Jo Ann McConnell also had a close call with a carjacker. She was driving with her 13-year-old son, Matthew, in December 2001, when she saw a man banging on the window of a car stopped in front of her. The man then ran up to her car and began banging on her window. McConnell's passenger door wasn't locked, so the man opened it and slid across toward the driver's seat. He tried to push McConnell out of the car. McConnell yelled at Matthew, who was sitting in the back. "Get out!" she shouted to him, and he quickly scrambled out.

Entangled in her seat belt, McConnell hung half in and half out of the car. The carjacker didn't care. He just stepped on the gas. McConnell tried to stay on her feet but the car was going too fast. She fell and was dragged along the road.

Luckily, three heroes came to her aid. Juan Carlos Meraz, Hector Meraz, and Javier Espinoza saw what was happening. These three men were driving in their pick-up truck. They raced ahead of McConnell's car and, in a quick move, forced her car into a parked car. The three men then leaped out of their truck, pulled the carjacker out of McConnell's car, and pinned him to the ground.

The Denver Police Department held a ceremony to honor the three men, none of whom spoke English. Said Police Chief Gerry Whitman, "This proves to you that heroism has no language barriers."

Jo Ann McConnell suffered a dislocated hip and some cuts and bruises as a result of being dragged along the road. But, as Matthew said, she owed her life to the Meraz brothers and Espinoza. "If they hadn't done what they did," said Matthew, "my mom probably wouldn't be here now."

If you have been timed while reading this article, enter your reading time below. Then turn to the Words-per-Minute Table on page 120 and look up your reading speed (words per minute). Enter your reading speed on the graph on page 121.

Reading Time: Selection 1

——————— : ———————
MINUTES   SECONDS

UNDERSTANDING IDEAS Circle the letter of the best answer.

1. **Which statement about Jo Ann McConnell's story belongs in the empty box?**

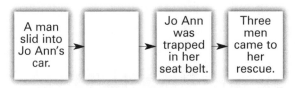

   A McConnell told her son to get out of the car and run.

   B The police had a ceremony for her rescuers.

   C Three men forced her car into a parked car.

   D A man banged on the window of the car in front of McConnell.

2. **According to police, what should you do if you are being carjacked?**

   F surrender the keys

   G fight the attackers

   H keep the keys

   J rescue your children

3. **Which statement about Katoria Lee's experience is correct?**

   A Her son David was awake the whole time.

   B The Wal-Mart parking lot was not well lit.

   C Three teenagers nearby paid no attention to her.

   D She was not shot.

4. **If the three men hadn't come to McConnell's aid, she would most likely have**

   F saved her son

   G died

   H jumped free

   J fought back

SUMMARIZE For each blank, choose the word that best completes the meaning of the paragraph.

shot	carjacked	
		fought
surprise	attacker	

Carjackers come out of nowhere and take

you by _____.

Katoria Lee was _____

late at night in a Wal-Mart parking lot. But she

_____ to get her son out of the

car. She was _____ in the

arm and back, but she rescued her son. Jo Ann

McConnell was dragged along the street by her

_____ until three men

forced the carjacker to a stop.

IF YOU WERE THERE Write a brief paragraph explaining what you would do if you were suddenly attacked by a carjacker. Be sure to include examples from the story to support your response.

_____

_____

_____

_____

_____

_____

Outrage in New York

Jrae Mason saw the two men approaching, but she had no idea who they were or what they wanted. Jrae was a mother of four and a grandmother of thirteen. On July 18, 1994, she was sitting on her front stoop in Harlem, in New York City. She was enjoying the warm summer evening and waiting for a friend to stop by. She didn't pay much attention to the two men rushing toward her. She didn't know that they were about to turn her lovely evening into a nightmare.

The men's names were Darren Fuentes and Javier Mulinary. They were "fugitive recovery agents," more commonly known as bounty hunters. Their job was to find people who had run away from criminal trials. Bounty hunters don't work for the police. They don't work for the courts, either. Instead, they work for private bail bond companies. These companies have to pay a lot of money if their clients run away from a trial. So the companies hire men like Fuentes and Mulinary to bring the suspects back.

None of this concerned Jrae Mason—or at least, she didn't think it did. She couldn't believe it when the two men grabbed her and slapped handcuffs on her. She was stunned when they said they were taking her back to Alabama to stand trial.

"Alabama?" she cried. "I've never even been to Alabama!"

Fuentes and Mulinary didn't believe her. They thought she was Audrey White Smith, a woman wanted on felony charges in Alabama. Jrae showed them several pieces of ID. Each one clearly identified her as Jrae Mason. But the bounty hunters were not convinced.

"They ignored my pleas," she later said. "They ignored my identification."

The men had a photo of Smith. Even though the picture showed a much shorter, thinner woman, they insisted it was Jrae. And so despite her protests, they shoved her into their car and drove off.

For the next several hours, the two men took Jrae all around the city as they made plans to transport her to Alabama. They went to three different police stations. At each one, Jrae tried to explain who she really was. No one listened. Officers at one station checked her fingerprints. These showed that she really was Jrae Mason. But the bounty hunters thought that was just an alias. They continued with their plans.

Fuentes and Mulinary loaded Jrae into the back of a rental car. Then they left and two new men took over. They were Wally Holliman and Robert Hall. Jrae still had handcuffs on her wrists. These new men took off her shoes and put her in leg irons, as well.

"It's just horrible," said Jrae. "I was told if I didn't shut up, they would … gag me and throw me in the trunk of the car. I kept protesting that I was not the person they were looking for."

Hour after hour, mile after mile, the two men drove south. Jrae, terrified, remained in the back seat.

"I was so afraid, I thought I might die on those back roads where there were no other vehicles," Jrae said. "And I knew in my heart that I had done nothing wrong, yet I had been abducted, chained, and dragged from my home in New York City through states I had never been in before."

After three days on the road, they arrived in Tuscaloosa, Alabama. Holliman and Hall took Jrae to the local jail. Here she finally found someone who would listen to her. The officers took a careful look at the photo of Smith. They measured Jrae's height and weight, comparing it with Smith's. "When we got to checking, it was obvious she wasn't Smith," said Deputy Chief Harry Montgomery. "We just told 'em, you better get that lady back to New York."

Reluctantly, Holliman and Hall agreed. They bought Jrae a $24 bus ticket back to New York. They took her to the station and sent her home alone.

After Jrae got home, she contacted a lawyer. She didn't want the bounty hunters to get away with their irresponsible and abusive treatment of her. Lawyer David Breitbart agreed that she had a case. Bounty hunters are allowed to seize people and return them to trial. But they have to make sure they seize the right person. In Jrae's case, they had made no effort to do that. "This is an outrage," Breitbart said. "The bounty hunters didn't care. The bonding company didn't care. The police didn't care. This was just a poor black woman who didn't matter to any of them."

The jury agreed with him. After hearing Jrae's story, they ordered the bail bond company to pay her $1.2 million.

If you have been timed while reading this article, enter your reading time below. Then turn to the Words-per-Minute Table on page 120 and look up your reading speed (words per minute). Enter your reading speed on the graph on page 121.

Reading Time: Selection 2

_____ : _____
MINUTES   SECONDS

UNDERSTANDING IDEAS Circle the letter of the best answer.

1. **How did Jrae Mason's nightmare begin?**

   A She was driven all the way to Alabama.

   B Two men put handcuffs on her and took her from her home.

   C She was told if she didn't shut up, she would be gagged.

   D She was taken to three different police stations.

2. **Jrae Mason was taken by the bounty hunters because she**

   F owed the bounty hunters money

   G had run away from a criminal trial

   H was wanted by a private bail bond company

   J looked somewhat like another woman wanted on felony charges

3. **Jrae Mason was finally allowed to go home when**

   A bounty hunters compared her to the photo of Audrey White

   B police officers in Alabama checked her height and weight

   C she showed the bounty hunters her identification

   D officers in New York checked her fingerprints

4. **Why did a judge award Jrae Mason $1.2 million?**

   F The bounty hunters wrongfully seized Jrae Mason.

   G The bounty hunters sent Jrae home alone on the bus.

   H Bounty hunters are not allowed to seize people from their homes.

   J The bounty hunters put her in handcuffs and leg irons.

SUMMARIZE For each blank, choose the word that best completes the meaning of the paragraph.

Alabama	felon	stoop
handcuffed	realized	police

On a summer night in 1994, Jrae Mason was sitting on her front _____ in New York City. Two men approached her and _____ her. She was taken to three different _____ stations in New York City. Then she was driven all the way to _____. She was thought to be a _____ named Audrey White. When she arrived in Alabama, police officers finally _____ she was not the right woman.

IF YOU WERE THERE Imagine that you are a bounty hunter in search of a wanted felon. Write a brief paragraph explaining the steps you would take to be sure you had the right person. Include examples from the story to support your response.

_____

_____

_____

_____

_____

USE CONTEXT CLUES When you read, you may find a word whose meaning is unfamiliar to you. When that happens, you can look up the word's meaning in the dictionary. You can also find out what the word means by looking for context clues. These are words or sentences that come before or after the word. Context clues can be synonyms or antonyms of the unfamiliar word. They may also be an example or definition of the unfamiliar word.

Read each excerpt from the stories you just read. Circle the letter with the best meaning of the underlined word.

1. **You could be stopped at a red light or parked in front of a convience store . . . You could even be in your own driveway when the attack <u>occurs</u>.**

   A happens

   B follows

   C prevents

   D surprises

2. **When she <u>emerged</u> from the store, however, a young man appeared and pointed a gun at her. Lee tried to run back inside the store.**

   F went into

   G walked through

   H came out of

   J hid under

3. **Katoria Lee survived her <u>ordeal</u> but said, "I'll never be the same." She underwent four operations and suffered from violent nightmares.**

   A fun vacation

   B painful memory

   C tough examination

   D difficult experience

4. **"It's just horrible," said Jrae. "I was told if I didn't shut up they would . . . <u>gag</u> me and throw me in the trunk of the car."**

   F ignore

   G prevent speaking

   H physically hurt

   J restrict movement

5. **After Jrae got home, she contacted a lawyer. She didn't want the bounty hunters to get away with their irresponsible and <u>abusive</u> treatment of her.**

   A insulting and hurtful

   B confusing and quiet

   C kind and generous

   D lazy and ignorant

PUT WORDS INTO CONTEXT Complete the paragraph using the underlined words from the exercise on this page.

A carjacking can be a very frightening

_____. It usually

_____ when you least expect it.

Imagine: you have just _____

from a store when a man jumps out and demands

your car keys. If you resist, he may become

_____. You may end up injured

or even dead.

PREFIXES A prefix is one or more letters added to the beginning of a word to change its meaning. For example, the prefix *non-* means "not." The word *toxic* means "poisonous." So, when you add the prefix *non-* to the word *toxic*, you get *nontoxic*, which means "not poisonous."

Use a dictionary to find the meaning of each prefix below. Match the prefix with its meaning on the right. Examples for each definition are included in italics. Write the letter of the correct definition on the line. **One of the definitons will be used twice.**

_____	**1.** auto-	**A**	not, the opposite of: *unhappy, disapprove*
_____	**2.** un-	**B**	across the other side of: *transcontinental*
_____	**3.** re-	**C**	again: *reattach*
_____	**4.** dis-	**D**	self-acting, automatic: *autopilot*
_____	**5.** mid-	**E**	before: *preview*
_____	**6.** trans-	**F**	the part in the middle: *midlife*
_____	**7.** pre-		

WRITE DEFINITIONS Underline the prefix and write the meaning of the following words in the space provided.

1. dis + located = dislocated

definition: _____

2. un + locked = unlocked

definition: _____

3. mid + day = midday

definition: _____

4. re + turn = return

definition: _____

5. trans + port = transport

definition: _____

6. pre + school = preschool

definition: _____

7. auto + mobile = automobile

definition: _____

ORGANIZE THE FACTS A summary retells the major points of the story. Minor details and examples are not included. To write a summary, first you must decide what the most important points are. You can do this by making a list. Then write a paragraph using the main points from your list. The paragraph is your summary.

Look at the major points listed under "Your Keys or Your Life." Fill in the missing information. Then list the major points of "Outrage in New York."

"Your Keys or Your Life"
1. Carjackers strike out of nowhere.
2. They can attack in a parking lot, at a red light, or even in your own driveway.
3. Police say you should always give up your keys immediately.
4. Katoria Lee gave up her keys but was shot anyway. She managed to rescue her son before her car was stolen.
5.

"Outrage in New York"
1. Jrae Mason was approached by two men while sitting on her front stoop.
2.
3.
4.
5.

COMPARE THE STORIES Using the major points listed above, write a brief paragraph summarizing "Outrage in New York."

_____

_____

_____

_____

_____

_____

MAKE PREDICTIONS You can make predictions, or educated guesses, based on what you already know. For example, you know that there is a traffic jam on the main highway every day between five and six o'clock in the evening. Based on this knowledge, you can reasonably predict that tomorrow's traffic will be the same way.

Read this passage, and answer the following questions based on what you know after reading the stories.

Hand Over the Keys

Beth Albright was on her way home. It was late, but she stopped at the grocery store to pick up breakfast for the next morning. She pulled into a parking spot and got out of her car. As she did, a man stepped out of the shadows. Beth could not see any weapon. "Give me the keys!" he said. Beth threw the keys as hard as she could across the parking lot and ran for the safety of the store.

---

1. **What do you predict the carjacker will do next?**

   A turn him or herself in

   B look for the keys

   C go shopping in the store

   D apologize to Beth

2. **What do you predict Beth would do if her attacker had a gun?**

   F scream loudly for help

   G try to run to the store

   H quickly hand over her car keys

   J throw the keys across the parking lot

3. **What do you predict Beth would do if she had a small child in the car?**

   A give the carjacker her keys

   B call the police

   C try to get the child out of the car

   D stay in the car with her child

JUDGE THE BASIS OF A PREDICTION For predictions to be reasonably accurate, they must be based on what you know as factual information. Choose the best answer.

1. **Which information helps you predict what Beth would have done if the attacker were armed?**

   A Police say your car is less important than your life.

   B Katoria called to nearby teens and was ignored.

   C An elderly man was able to fight off his attackers.

   D Jo Ann was saved by three heroic men.

2. **Which statement helps you predict what Beth would do if there was a child in her car?**

   F A senior citizen fought with two carjackers and won.

   G Katoria and Jo Ann fought to free their children.

   H Jo Ann McConnell was dragged along the road.

   J Katoria Lee was shot in the arm and back.

PREDICT WHAT YOU WOULD DO Write a brief paragraph explaining what you would do if you were surprised by a carjacker. Tell also what you would not do. Use examples from the stories you just read to explain your decisions.

_____

_____

_____

_____

_____

SELECTION 1

"A Part of Me Died"

"Get off the highest peaks by 11:00 A.M." That's the warning all hikers get in the Rocky Mountains during the summer. Park rangers issue this warning because they know that thunderstorms usually occur in the afternoon. And a mountain peak is definitely not a good place to be during a thunderstorm.

There are other bad places. A golf course is dangerous. Being in a metal boat in the middle of a lake isn't too safe, either. But the worst place to be is on the top on a mountain. Lightning will usually hit the tallest thing around. If you're standing on the peak of a high mountain, *you* are the tallest thing around. You don't even have to be on the peak to be in danger. Any place in the open can be bad. In the Rockies, that means any spot above the tree line.

Lightning is a form of electricity. Metal pipes and wires are good conductors of electricity. Water is another fine conductor. (You don't want to be holding a metal baseball bat or swimming in a lake in a thunderstorm.) Humans are also good conductors of electricity. That is because our nerves, blood, and muscles are made mostly of water. About one hundred Americans are killed by lightning each year. They are not vaporized or turned into ashes. They die from heart attacks. Their hearts are stopped by the huge surge of electricity that lightning sends through their bodies.

Daniel Clark knew all this. He knew he shouldn't be high in the mountains after 11:00 A.M. But on August 14, 1998, he had no choice. Clark was an emergency medical technician. On that day, he got a message that a hiker on Colorado's Twin Sisters Mountain was very ill. The man needed assistance. So around noon, Clark was making his way toward the victim. Suddenly, a bolt of lightning struck fifteen feet from him. It knocked him down and blew out his left eardrum.

Dazed, Clark got back up. He looked around. Rain and hail pelted him. He feared another bolt of lightning. So he fell to the ground and curled into a ball. He knew that was his best hope. But it wasn't good enough. All at once he saw a bright light. A "hot flash" raced through his body. Clark later said, "I think the biggest thing about being struck by lightning was that part of me died, part of my old self. It changed my life forever."

This second bolt knocked Clark out for forty minutes. He survived. But he was permanently injured. Doctors fixed his left eardrum. Still, he lost some hearing in both ears. The strike affected his memory. It also left him suffering from headaches and depression. Before he was struck by lightning, Clark loved a good thunderstorm. "I still enjoy it from a distance," he said. "But if it's close, it scares the hell out of me."

Unlike Daniel Clark, Steve Marshburn wasn't out in the open when he was hit by lightning. He was in a nice, solid bank. On November 25, 1970, Marshburn was working at the drive-through window of a bank in Swanboro, North Carolina. Lightning struck some electrical wires ten miles away. These wires ran to the speaker that Marshburn held. The lightning traveled along the wires and right into Marshburn's spine.

"It felt like someone hit me in the back with a wooden baseball bat," Marshburn said. "It chipped a bone in my spine where it entered. It hurt so bad, I couldn't believe it."

Like Daniel Clark, Steve Marshburn suffered injuries that changed his life forever. He suffered from chronic pain. He had muscle cramps and skin rashes. His vision became blurry. He developed strange food allergies. He could no longer eat hamburgers or steak. If he did, his throat would swell up. Doctors operated on him more than two dozen times in an effort to restore his health.

What happened to Marshburn was a freak accident. But it shows the awesome power of lightning. Lightning can reach temperatures as high as 50,000 degrees Fahrenheit. So thunderstorms may be fun to watch—provided you keep a safe distance. Experts say everyone should follow the 30-30 rule. If there is less than 30 seconds between the flash of lightning and the sound of thunder, you are in danger. Find a safe place fast. Before leaving that spot, make sure there has been no lightning for 30 minutes. If you do this, you probably won't become a victim of lightning.

If you have been timed while reading this article, enter your reading time below. Then turn to the Words-per-Minute Table on page 120 and look up your reading speed (words per minute). Enter your reading speed on the graph on page 121.

Reading Time: Selection 1

_____ : _____

MINUTES   SECONDS

UNDERSTANDING IDEAS Circle the letter of the best answer.

1. **Which picture shows the WORST place to be during a thunderstorm?**

1. golf course   **2.** metal boat in the middle of a lake

3. top of a mountain   **4.** inside of a car

   A Picture 1
   B Picture 2
   C Picture 3
   D Picture 4

2. **According to the article, when people are killed by lightning, what actually causes their deaths?**
   F They have heart attacks.
   G They are vaporized.
   H They choke to death.
   J They turn to ashes.

3. **Which statement about Steve Marshburn's experience is correct?**
   A He lost hearing in both ears.
   B He forgot to wear rubber shoes.
   C He was hit by lightning on top of a mountain.
   D He was hit by lightning while working in a bank.

4. **All of the following are injuries people got from being hit by lightning EXCEPT**
   F loss of hearing
   G a stomach virus
   H muscle cramps
   J strange food allergies

SUMMARIZE For each blank, choose the word that best completes the meaning of the paragraph.

tallest	attacks	hearing
curl	distance	allergies

Thunderstorms can be fun to watch from a

_____. If you are caught

outside in a thunderstorm, you should

_____ up into a ball. Lightning

strikes the _____ thing around.

If you are hit by lightning, you may lose your

_____. Some people hit by

lightning develop strange _____

to food. Others have heart _____

and die.

IF YOU WERE THERE Write a brief paragraph explaining what you would do if you were caught out in the open during a thunderstorm. Be sure to include examples from the story to support your response.

_____

_____

_____

_____

Lightning Girl

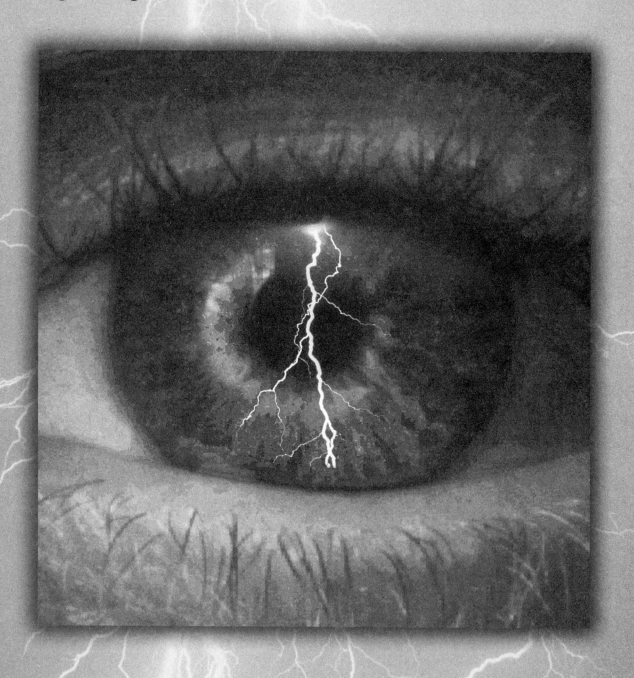

Their tickets read: "Rain or Shine." So no one wanted to leave when storm clouds gathered over Washington, D.C. As one man later said, most people didn't want to go home because of what looked like "a passing shower."

It was June 13, 1998, and more than 66,000 people had crowded into the RFK Stadium. They had come to enjoy a concert featuring some of the biggest names in rock music. The concert was a benefit performance to help the people of Tibet. And despite the threatening skies, most people weren't worried.

But suddenly, even before it began to rain, a bolt of lightning streaked across the sky and hit the stadium. Said one woman, "It sounded like a bomb went off. The ground shook. Everything just shook."

"The top of my head felt like it was on fire," said a man who suffered minor injuries.

The bolt hit 16-year-old Tiffani Vannoy. "I felt a shock through my legs," she said. "My legs were tingly. I was stumbling around because I was dizzy." Luckily, Tiffani's injuries turned out to be minor.

The lightning seemed to save most of its power for a 25-year-old law student named Lysa Selfon. Lysa and her sister, Amanda, were walking through the grandstand to meet friends when the lightning struck. The bolt knocked both of them to the floor. As Amanda scrambled to her feet, she saw Lysa still lying in the aisle. "Lysa," she cried, "you okay?"

But Lysa didn't respond. She was lying on her chest with her head twisted to the side. A trickle of blood ran out of her mouth. Her skin had turned ash-white. Amanda began screaming for help. People rushed to her aid. One was a doctor named Jamshed Zuberi. Another one was John Shaw, an emergency room technician. Medics on duty for the concert also came to help.

Zuberi and Shaw rolled Lysa onto her back. They saw burn holes in the front of her T-shirt. There was blood everywhere. Lysa had no pulse at all. She wasn't breathing. "Her body was like a rag doll," said Amanda. "No life in it at all."

Zuberi and Shaw realized they had to do something fast or Lysa would surely die. They began thumping her chest and doing mouth-to-mouth resuscitation. By now it was raining hard. Dozens of bystanders crowded around. Several of them were screaming. After a couple of minutes, Zuberi and Shaw put Lysa onto a stretcher. They moved her to a nearby dugout where it was quieter and they had more room to work.

In the dugout, Zuberi and Shaw saw that Lysa's neck was swelling from the burns she had sustained. Soon her airway would be closed off. They stuck a tube down her throat to keep it open, and continued squeezing oxygen into her lungs. By this time, her heartbeat had been stopped for more than five minutes. Two or three more minutes and there would be no hope—she would suffer irreversible brain damage. Fortunately, however, their efforts finally succeeded. Shaw felt a pulse. "It felt like it took forever," he later said. "But when you feel that pulse, it's a rush like you've never experienced before."

Lysa was alive, but she had suffered serious injuries. She had mangled her lip and damaged her nose when she fell. She had also chipped three teeth. In addition, the lightning itself had done extensive damage to her body. Apparently it had struck her in the head and had then run down her right side and exited from her right hip. It had left her with second and third-degree burns over 20 percent of her body. Most of these were on her face, neck, and chest. It had blown a hole in her right eardrum, which would affect her balance and make it hard for her to walk without help. It had also done damage to the nerves in her arms, which would make it hard for her to write or type. Later doctors would also discover that it had affected her short-term memory.

In the end, however, it was the shutdown of Lysa's heart that nearly killed her. The shock from the lightning bolt had made her heart stop beating. If Zuberi and Shaw hadn't acted so fast, she would have died. "She's incredibly lucky," said Marion Jordon, director of the Washington Hospital Center's burn center. "She has survived what could have been a fatal injury."

Lysa's friends started calling her "Lightning Girl." But Lysa Selfon had no memory of being hit. She remembered seeing the Dave Matthews Band. "I saw a little bit of Herbie Hancock. And that's all I know."

Why was she the only one seriously hurt out of 66,000 fans? No one knows. She wasn't the tallest person around. She wasn't holding onto a metal railing or umbrella. Lightning is an unpredictable force of nature. Lysa Selfon accepted the accident as part of life. She said, "I've had a couple of car accidents, a couple of skiing accidents. Some people have illnesses. I have accidents." So Lysa didn't curse the gods or get depressed. She wanted to get on with the rest of her life. She later said, "Bad things happen to good people, and you move on."

If you have been timed while reading this article, enter your reading time below. Then turn to the Words-per-Minute Table on page 120 and look up your reading speed (words per minute). Enter your reading speed on the graph on page 121.

Reading Time: Selection 2

_____ : _____
MINUTES   SECONDS

UNDERSTANDING IDEAS Circle the letter of the best answer.

1. Which statement belongs in the empty box?

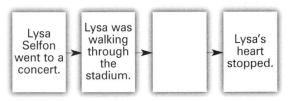

A The lightning affected Lysa's short-term memory.

B Lysa's friends called her "Lightning Girl."

C Lysa went to a benefit concert.

D Lightning struck and knocked Lysa to the ground.

2. Which step did Shaw and Zuberi take to keep Lysa Selfon alive?

F thumping her chest

G mouth-to-mouth resuscitation

H keeping her throat open with a tube

J all of the above

3. Lysa nearly died when her

A teeth were chipped

B heart stopped beating

C mouth was bleeding

D eardrum was blown out

4. What conclusion can you draw about Lysa?

F She tends to accept accidents as part of life.

G She knows she would not survive any future accidents.

H She gets depressed every time she is in an accident.

J She appreciates the attention she gets during an accident.

SUMMARIZE For each blank, choose the word that best completes the meaning of the paragraph.

injured	sister	rain
concert	stopped	lightning

In June 1998, 66,000 people went to a benefit

_____ at RFK Stadium. It was

about to _____, but no one

wanted to go home. Then Tiffani Vannoy was

hit by _____. She was not

seriously _____. Lysa Selfon and

her _____ were also hit by a bolt

of lightning. Lysa's heart _____

beating and she nearly died.

IF YOU WERE THERE Imagine that you are with someone when he or she is hit by lightning. Write a brief paragraph explaining the steps you would take to save his or her life. Be sure to include examples from the story to support your response.

_____

_____

_____

_____

_____

USE CONTEXT CLUES When you read, you may find a word whose meaning is unfamiliar to you. When that happens, you can look up the word's meaning in the dictionary. You can also find out what the word means by looking for context clues. These are words or sentences that come before or after the word. Context clues can be synonyms or antonyms of the unfamiliar word. They may also be an example or definition of the unfamiliar word.

Read each excerpt from the stories you just read. Circle the letter with the best meaning of the underlined word.

1. "Get off the highest <u>peaks</u> by 11:00 A.M." That's the warning all hikers get in the Rocky Mountains during the summer.

   A dense forest

   B highest point

   C open space

   D tall building

2. Humans are also fine conductors of electricty. . . . Their hearts are stopped by the huge <u>surge</u> of electricity that lightning sends through their bodies.

   F drip

   G light

   H rush

   J trickle

3. He survived. But he was <u>permanently</u> injured. . . . The strike affected his memory. It also left him suffering from headaches and depression.

   A fatally

   B for a short period of time

   C forever

   D unusually

4. Zuberi and Shaw realized they had to do something fast or Lysa would surely die. They began thumping her chest and doing mouth-to-mouth <u>resuscitation</u>.

   F injuring

   G reviving

   H operating

   J beating

5. In the dugout, Zuberi and Shaw saw that Lysa's neck was swelling from the burns she had <u>sustained</u>. Soon her airway would be closed off.

   A blocked

   B created

   C injured

   D suffered

PUT WORDS INTO CONTEXT Complete the paragraph using the underlined words from the exercise on this page.

The highest _____ of mountains

can be very dangerous during a thunderstorm.

When lightning strikes, it causes a

_____ of electricity to race through

the body. Lightning victims have _____

a variety of injuries. Some even require mouth-to-mouth

_____ to get their hearts to start

beating again. Sometimes victims from a lightning strike

are _____ injured.

MULTIPLE MEANINGS Most words have many different meanings. You can determine the correct meaning of the word by seeing how the word is used in a sentence.

Read the definitions of each word. On the line, write the meaning of the underlined word as it is used in the sentence.

> **conductor:** **1.** a material that permits an electric current to flow easily **2.** a collector of fares on public transportation (i.e. train)

1. Water is another fine <u>conductor</u>.

_____

2. The <u>conductor</u> took our tickets as we boarded the train.

_____

> **speaker:** **1.** a person talking **2.** reproduces sound for a radio

3. These wires ran to the <u>speaker</u> that Marshburn held.

_____

4. The guest <u>speaker</u> for the assembly gave a talk about applying to college.

_____

> **benefit:** **1.** a payment made in accordance with a wage agreement or insurance policy **2.** a performance or event to raise funds

5. The concert was a <u>benefit</u> performance to help the people of Tibet.

_____

6. My new job has an excellent health <u>benefit</u> program.

_____

> **minor:** **1.** less important, not serious **2.** person under age **3.** a mode of music **4.** course of study

7. Tiffani's injuries turned out to be <u>minor</u>.

_____

8. Jack will still be a <u>minor</u> until his eighteenth birthday.

_____

> **lying:** **1.** not telling the truth **2.** stretched out flat

9. She was <u>lying</u> on her chest with her head twisted to the side.

_____

10. Rachel knew the man was <u>lying</u> when he said he wasn't hurt.

_____

ORGANIZE THE FACTS The two stories you read in this unit are alike in some ways and different in other ways. A Venn diagram can show how they are alike and different. Look at the Venn diagram below. Then choose the best answer to each question.

"A PART OF ME DIED"
Describes two less serious incidents

BOTH
about being struck by lightning

"LIGHTNING GIRL"
Describes one serious incident

1. **Which of the following details about being struck by lightning does NOT belong in the oval marked "BOTH"?**

   A bones and teeth are chipped

   B heart stops beating

   C eardrums are damaged

   D memory is affected

2. **Which detail does NOT belong in the oval marked "A Part of Me Died"?**

   F Daniel Clark was out in the open when lightning struck him.

   G Lightning traveled along wires into Steve Marshburn's spine.

   H The victim needed several operations.

   J There were burn holes in the front of Lysa's T-shirt.

3. **Which detail does NOT belong in the oval marked "Lightning Girl"?**

   A The main character developed food allergies.

   B The main character was with her sister when the accident occurred.

   C The victim wasn't holding anything metal.

   D A doctor and an ER technician quickly helped.

PROVE THE COMPARISON AND CONTRAST Compare and contrast the two stories by writing a short paragraph to support the following topic sentences.

The two stories are alike in some ways.

_____

_____

_____

_____

_____

_____

The two stories are different in some ways.

_____

_____

_____

_____

_____

FACT AND OPINION A statement of fact is one that you can prove to be true. An opinion is a belief or conclusion that is still open to debate.

Read this passage about being struck by lightning. Then choose the best answer to each question.

[1] Each year, nearly one hundred Americans are killed by lightning. [2] Men are struck by lightning four times more often than women. [3] Why does lightning strike men more often? [4] Perhaps it's because men are more often caught outside holding a metal object during a storm.

1. **Which sentence states a fact about who is struck by lightning most often?**

    A Sentence 1

    B Sentence 2

    C Sentence 3

    D Sentence 4

2. **Which sentence from the passage states an opinion about being struck by lightning?**

    F Sentence 1

    G Sentence 2

    H Sentence 3

    J Sentence 4

3. **Which of the following statements is an opinion?**

    A Both men and women have been struck by lightning.

    B Metal objects attract lightning.

    C People should not touch metal during a thunderstorm.

    D Women are struck by lightning less than men because they don't like spending time outside.

JUDGE THE EVIDENCE To convince a reader to agree to an opinion, the writer often provides evidence. The reader has to judge if the evidence is adequate to support the opinion. Choose the best answer.

1. **Which statement supports the opinion that a mountain peak is not a good place to be during a thunderstorm?**

    A Lightning can reach very high temperatures.

    B Metal pipes and wires conduct electricity.

    C Lightning usually hits the tallest thing around.

    D Thunderstorms usually occur in the afternoon.

2. **Which statement best supports the opinion that lightning causes unusual injuries?**

    F Steve Marshburn could no longer eat hamburgers or steak.

    G Lightning is so hot it often burns victims.

    H Victims often lose part of their hearing.

    J Lysa was struck, but her sister Amanda was not.

YOUR OPINION Write a brief paragraph expressing your opinion about the injuries caused by lightning. Support your opinion with evidence from the stories you have read.

_____

_____

_____

_____

Hysteria over Halley's Comet

Scientists agree: A comet is nothing more than a "dirty snowball." It is made up of ice, dust, and frozen gases. It usually isn't large—just a few miles across. It goes around the sun like the earth, but in a very elongated orbit. It comes close to the sun and then disappears into deep space for a long time. Some comets don't come back for thousands of years. A few, like Halley's comet, come back much more often. Halley's comet flashes through the sky every 75 years or so.

While a comet may be small, it can put on a dazzling show. As it approaches the sun, it heats up. Bits of burning gas and dust break away. This causes the comet to glow. It looks much larger than it is. The heat of a comet gives it a brilliant tail that can extend for millions of miles. So a comet appears to blaze across the sky.

Comets have amazed and terrified people for thousands of years. Today we know what comets are. But imagine if you *didn't* know. Imagine that you're living on the earth 500 or 1000 years ago. One night you glance up and see a blazing object streaking across the sky. It wasn't there last night. To you, the bright object seems to have come from nowhere. It has come without warning. In a few days it is gone, and you never see it again.

What do you think? We know what people who lived long ago actually did think about comets. They thought comets were messages from God. Most people believed they were evil omens. Often comets were blamed for earthquakes, floods, droughts, and wars. The Chinese said that comets were like brooms. God was sweeping evil out of the heavens.

In A.D. 66, according to a Jewish historian, Halley's comet "hung like a sword in the sky." Just four years later, the city of Jerusalem was destroyed by the Roman army. Many people believed the comet was a warning that the city was doomed. In 1066, the comet reappeared. That was the year William the Conqueror invaded England. He defeated the Saxons in the Battle of Hastings. Scenes from the battle were woven into the famous Bayeux tapestry. Halley's comet was stitched into the tapestry, too. The Saxons believed the comet caused their defeat. They believed it also caused the death of their king, Harold.

In 1456, people blamed Halley's comet for earthquakes. They blamed it for a strange red rain that fell. They even blamed it for the birth of two-headed animals. Pope Callixtus III excommunicated the comet, saying it was a tool of the devil. Some people believed that Halley's comet caused the massacre at the Alamo in 1835. They also blamed it for a destructive fire in New York City and for more than half a dozen wars. One group was so sure the comet signaled the end of the world that they refused to harvest their crops.

By 1910, most people understood the truth about comets. They no longer saw them as harbingers of disaster. Still, Halley's comet caused a small panic when it returned that year. Scientists predicted that the earth would pass through the tail of the comet. Although this posed no danger to humans, the news terrified some people. They believed the gases in the tail would poison the air, killing everyone on the earth. Others believed the tail would turn the air into nitrous oxide, or laughing gas. Everyone would die laughing.

Newspapers helped to spark the panic. They printed stories about the dangers that people faced. Scientists tried to tell the truth, but their view didn't sell newspapers. Many people got only the bad news. Some bought gas masks. Others bought "comet pills" from entrepreneurs eager to make money out of people's fears. The pills sold extremely well because people wanted to believe they would work.

The earth did pass through the tail. All the people who had taken the pills lived. But then, so did everyone else. The comet produced some weird lights in the sky, but that's all it did. No one was poisoned. No one died laughing. The real wonder of

Halley's comet was the sight of it shooting across the heavens. Its fiery tail covered about one tenth of the night sky.

Halley's comet came back again in 1910, the comet had come within 14 million miles of the earth. This time it got no closer than 39 million miles. Maybe it will do better next time. Halley's comet is due back in 2061. Comet pills, anyone?

If you have been timed while reading this article, enter your reading time below. Then turn to the Words-per-Minute Table on page 120 and look up your reading speed (words per minute). Enter your reading speed on the graph on page 121.

Reading Time: Selection 1

_____ : _____
MINUTES   SECONDS

UNDERSTANDING IDEAS Circle the letter of the best answer.

1. Which picture shows what a comet looks like?

1.   2.

3.   4.

   A Picture 1

   B Picture 2

   C Picture 3

   D Picture 4

2. According to the article, people who lived long ago thought comets were

   F evil omens

   G dirty snowballs

   H alien spaceships

   J friendly visitors

3. All of the following events were blamed on the appearance of Halley's comet EXCEPT

   A the massacre at the Alamo in 1865

   B the appointment of Pope Callixtus III

   C the Roman army's destruction of the city of Jerusalem

   D William the Conqueror's defeat of the Saxons in the Battle of Hastings

4. What did people think would happen when the earth passed through the comet's tail?

   F A strange red rain would fall.

   G Two-headed animals would be born.

   H Poisonous gases would kill everyone on the earth.

   J New York City would be destroyed in a fire.

SUMMARIZE For each blank, choose the word that best completes the meaning of the paragraph.

wars	comet	lights
gases	streak	blamed

Comets are made up of ice, dust, and frozen

_____. They have brilliant tails that

_____ across the sky. Over the years,

people have _____ comets for many

disasters. Comets were blamed for earthquakes, floods,

and even _____. Some people even

thought a _____ would cause the end

of the world. In reality, comets do nothing but make some

strange _____ in the sky.

IF YOU WERE THERE Write a brief paragraph explaining what you would think if you saw a comet and didn't know what it was. Be sure to include examples from the story to support your response.

_____

_____

_____

_____

_____

_____

Hale-Bopp Fantasy

It was a stunning sight. Amateur astronomer Chuck Shramek was both puzzled and amazed. On November 14, 1996, Shramek was scanning the sky with his telescope, looking for the Hale-Bopp comet. This comet had first been seen in 1995 by astronomers Alan Hale and Thomas Bopp. That's how it got its name. But what surprised Shramek wasn't Hale-Bopp. It was a huge shining object trailing behind the comet. Shramek couldn't figure out what it was. He took pictures. Then he checked his electronic star chart. He found no planet or star in that spot. At last, Shramek decided that what he was seeing was a UFO.

Shramek spread the news by going on talk radio. Soon everyone was discussing it. People posted countless messages about it on the Internet. Within a couple of days, however, experts discovered the truth. The object was just a star. There was nothing special about it. When checking his star chart, Shramek had made a mistake. He hadn't used the right settings. If he had, he would have seen the star.

Facts are facts. But rumors are often stronger. Even Alan Hale couldn't stop them. Hale wanted people to forget the idea of a UFO and "enjoy the beauty of the comet for its own sake." But some people didn't want to hear that. They wanted to believe the rumors. They wanted the comet to be much more than it really was.

"I've had people tell me that Hale-Bopp is 'an angel from God,' and I even had one person say that Hale-Bopp is God," said Hale. Some people thought the comet was "going to drop off a bunch of poisonous gas in our atmosphere and knock us all off." Others thought the shining object trailing the comet was an "alien spacecraft, four times larger than the earth" and "under intelligent control." Some of these true believers attacked Hale. They called him a "traitor to the earth." They accused him of hiding the truth.

These were just words. But one group of people acted on their beliefs. The group was called Heaven's Gate. Marshall Applewhite, nicknamed Do, was its leader. He believed the appearance of Hale-Bopp was "the sign we have been waiting for." He declared the object behind the comet was indeed a spaceship and was piloted by aliens that were a "level above human." One of these aliens, Do said, was named Ti. In a former life as a human being, she had been Bonnie Lu Trusdale. She and Do had founded Heaven's Gate together. But she had died in 1985. To Do, that meant she was already on the "level above human." He believed she was now coming back to get him.

Do expected the spaceship to take him and his followers to a new world in the real "Kingdom of Heaven." He wrote, "We fully desire, expect, and look forward to boarding a spacecraft from the Next Level very soon." First, however, they had to get ready. Do and the other members of Heaven's Gate needed to get rid of their physical bodies. Only then would their spiritual bodies be free to join the aliens.

Do told his followers they would have to commit suicide. Thirty-eight members of the cult agreed to do so. These people were not teenagers or runaways. They were educated adults ranging in age from 26 to 72. Still, they went along with Do's plan. On March 23, 1997, they gathered at a mansion in San Diego. They laid out beds in a neat row. Fifteen died that first day. They ate pudding spiked with poison and drank some vodka. Then they put plastic bags over their heads. They all died from suffocation. Each one wore black pants and brand-new black sneakers. They all packed a suitcase that stood next to their bed. Each one had an ID in one pocket and a five-dollar bill and some coins in another. The next day, another fifteen members "left their bodies." On the third day, the last nine died.

In all, 39 people, including Do, killed themselves. The news of the mass suicide shocked people. Alice Maeder was horrified to learn that her daughter, Gail, was among the dead. Gail had been just 28 years old. Maeder didn't think of it as 39 suicides. With her voice shaking with rage, she said, "There was one suicide [Do's] and 38 murders. This has nothing to do with religion. It is about mind control."

The news of the Heaven's Gate suicides saddened Alan Hale. A few days after the suicides, he met with reporters. He offered his sympathy to the families of the dead. Then he repeated his belief that the comet was "a beautiful object." He said, "It's lovely. It's one of the most magnificent celestial objects you will ever see." But he added that, despite its beauty, the comet had no power either to hurt or to help people. "All it is," he said, "is a dirty snowball that's orbiting the sun."

If you have been timed while reading this article, enter your reading time below. Then turn to the Words-per-Minute Table on page 120 and look up your reading speed (words per minute). Enter your reading speed on the graph on page 121.

Reading Time: Selection 2

_____ : _____
MINUTES   SECONDS

UNDERSTANDING IDEAS Circle the letter of the best answer.

1. **What did amateur astronomer Chuck Shramek actually see in Hale-Bopp's tail?**

   A a planet

   B a comet

   C a UFO

   D a star

2. **Rumors spread that Hale-Bopp was all of the following EXCEPT**

   F an angel from God

   G simply a comet

   H dropping off poisonous gas

   J carrying an alien spacecraft

3. **Which statement belongs in the empty box?**

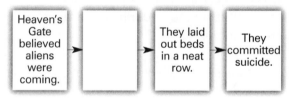

   A They gathered in San Diego to prepare to join the aliens.

   B In all, 39 people killed themselves.

   C Chuck Shramek realized he had made a mistake.

   D Bonnie Lu Trusdale died in 1985.

4. **Alan Hale's reaction to the Heaven's Gate suicides was**

   F to claim responsibility for the deaths

   G to insist the comet was a UFO

   H to express sadness and sympathy for the families of the dead

   J to admit he was a "traitor to the earth" trying to hide the truth

SUMMARIZE For each blank, choose the word that best completes the meaning of the paragraph.

alien	star	tail
cult	join	

Chuck Shramek thought he saw an object in the

_____ of the Hale-Bopp comet.

Rumors began to fly, even after the object was

discovered to be a _____.

Some people thought the object was an

_____ spacecraft. The

_____ group Heaven's Gate

believed the appearance of Hale-Bopp was a sign. They

prepared to _____ the aliens on

their ship.

IF YOU WERE THERE Write a brief paragraph explaining what you would do if a friend joined Heaven's Gate. How would you talk him or her out of dying to join the "aliens"? Be sure to include examples from the story to support your response.

_____

_____

_____

_____

_____

USE CONTEXT CLUES When you read, you may find a word whose meaning is unfamiliar to you. When that happens, you can look up the word's meaning in the dictionary. You can also find out what the word means by looking for context clues. These are words or sentences that come before or after the word. Context clues can be synonyms or antonyms of the unfamiliar word. They may also be an example or definition of the unfamiliar word.

Read each excerpt from the stories you just read. Circle the letter with the best meaning of the underlined word.

1. **They also blamed it [Haley's comet] for a destructive fire in New York City and for more than half a dozen wars. . . . By 1910, most people understood the truth about comets. They no longer saw them as harbingers of disaster.**

   A trails
   B signs
   C lights
   D denials

2. **Others bought "comet pills" from entrepreneurs eager to make money out of people's fears. The pills sold extremely well because people wanted to believe they would work.**

   F doctors
   G pharmacists
   H businessmen
   J ministers

3. **Amateur astronomer Chuck Shramek was both puzzled and amazed. On November 14, 1996, Shramek was scanning the sky with his telescope, looking for the Hale-Bopp comet.**

   A civil engineer
   B religious leader
   C television reporter
   D person who studies stars

4. **Do told his followers they would have to commit suicide. Thirty-eight members of the cult agreed to do so.**

   F religious group
   G college class
   H alien spaceship
   J scientific group

5. **Then he repeated his belief that the comet was "a beautiful object." He said, "It's lovely. It's one of the most magnificent celestial objects you will ever see."**

   A dangerous
   B heavenly
   C usual
   D earthly

PUT WORDS INTO CONTEXT Complete the paragraph using the underlined words from the exercise on this page.

Over time, people have had a variety of opinions about the _____ objects known as comets. Long ago, comets were seen as _____ of disaster. Eager to make money, _____ built businesses around people's fears. Even today, the occasional _____ is formed around the belief that comets are somehow connected with God or heaven. But to an _____, a comet will always be simply a beautiful object in the sky.

GREEK AND LATIN ROOTS As you have learned, one way of finding out the meaning of a word is by looking for its root. Many words we use in English have Latin and Greek roots. The chart below shows some examples.

Root	Origin	Meaning	Examples
dic	Latin	say, speak	diction, predict, dictates
milli	Latin	thousands	millions, millimeter, millionaire
sign	Latin	sign	signals, designate, signifies
dec, deca, deka	Greek	ten	decade, decimal, decameter
mono	Greek	one	monopolize, monotone, monogram
physi	Greek	nature	physics, physical, physician

For numbers 1 through 6, read the complete paragraph. For each numbered blank, refer to the corresponding answer at the right. Use the chart to choose the word that best completes the paragraph.

Many people believe the appearance of a comet

(1) _____ something important. In earlier times, the comet was thought to

(2) _____ bad things to come. But when Alan Hale and Thomas Bopp discovered a comet in 1995, they thought it was beautiful. A year later Chuck Shramek thought he saw a UFO in the comet's tail. Scientists said the object was a star, but by then,

the rumors had already begun to

(3) _____ the papers. The cult group Heaven's Gate believed this was the sign they were waiting for. The group's leader believed that co-founder Bonnie Lu, who had died more than a

(4) _____ ago, was returning to bring them to a new life. The group planned to commit suicide in order to get rid of their

(5) _____ bodies. In three days, all 39 cult members killed themselves. Alan Hale was saddened that an object (6)_____ of miles away could affect human lives in this way.

1. **A** dictate
   B physics
   C designate
   D signals

2. **F** predict
   G millimeter
   H monotone
   J physician

3. **A** decade
   B monopolize
   C physics
   D signifies

4. **F** decade
   G physical
   H millionaire
   J monotone

5. **A** decimal
   B dictate
   C millimeter
   D physical

6. **F** decameter
   G diction
   H millions
   J monogram

ORGANIZE THE FACTS To understand a passage, you should ask questions about the text before, during, and after reading, and then look for answers. While you are reading, know how and where to look for answers to questions. Sometimes the answer might be stated directly in the passage. Other times you need to put ideas or information together to come up with the answer. Then sometimes the answer may not be in the passage at all but may be something you already know.

Look at the chart below. Then answer the questions on the right.

Question-Answer Relationships	
Question	**How to Answer**
• Who discovered the Hale-Bopp comet?	Question words such as *who, where,* and *when* usually indicate that the answer is right there in the passage.
• What gives the comet a brilliant tail?	The question words *what* and *why* sometimes require you to think and to search passages.
• Why are comets so unusual?	A general question like this is about something you probably know. You can come up with the answer on your own.
• How do you think people would react if they were told the earth would pass through the tail of a comet today?	A question that asks what you think requires you to use what you already know and what the author tells you.

1. **Which question can you answer by looking for a direct statement from the story?**

   A When is Halley's comet due to come back?

   B Why did people think comets were messages from God?

   C How did entrepreneurs sell so many comet pills in 1910?

   D What caused the Heaven's Gate group to commit suicide?

2. **Which question can you answer by thinking and searching?**

   F When did Halley's comet last appear?

   G When was Hale-Bopp first discovered?

   H Who were the co-founders of Heaven's Gate?

   J What were the rumors about Hale-Bopp?

3. **Which question requires you to combine what you already know from experience with what the author tells you?**

   A What did Alan Hale say about the Hale-Bopp comet?

   B What were the rumors about Hale-Bopp?

   C What disasters have been blamed on Halley's comet?

   D How do you think rumors about the comet spread so quickly in 1910?

WRITE YOUR OWN QUESTIONS Write two questions about each of the stories in this unit. For each question, explain how you would find the answer.

_____

_____

_____

_____

_____

VERIFYING EVIDENCE As a reader, it's up to you to weigh the evidence being offered in any piece of writing. When the author has written to inform or persuade, you must verify or confirm the evidence being offered and judge how believable that evidence is. Read the article below and then choose the best answer for each question.

[1] Author Mark Twain was born in Florida, Missouri, on November 30, 1835. [2] During that time, Halley's comet was said to be visible in the sky. [3] Mark Twain knew he was born during the time of the comet. [4] He predicted that he would die when the comet again became visible. [5] He said, "I came in with Halley's Comet in 1835. [6] It is coming again next year, and I expect to go out with it." [7] Mark Twain died on April 21, 1910. [8] When he died, it is said that Halley's comet was once again visible in the sky. [9] Astronomers say this is possible, but Twain was not the only one to come and go with the comet. [10] Anybody born in the northern hemisphere at least six weeks before or after mid-October 1835, and dying within the month before or after May 18, 1910, can share Twain's comet legend.

1. **Which fact can you verify by reading Mark Twain's biography?**

   A the dates of his birth and death

   B how people in Missouri responded to the comet

   C how many times Halley's Comet has appeared

   D what astronomers have said about Halley's Comet

2. **Which sentences offer the most convincing evidence that Mark Twain was born and died while Halley's Comet was visible?**

   F Sentences 1 and 2

   G Sentences 3 and 4

   H Sentences 5 and 6

   J Sentences 9 and 10

JUDGE THE EVIDENCE To persuade the reader of an opinion or story, the author often provides evidence. It is up to the reader to judge whether the evidence presented is believable or not.

1. **Which statement supports the opinion that comets are harmless?**

   A Scientists tried to tell the truth, but their view didn't sell newspapers.

   B The comet produced weird lights in the sky, but that's all it did.

   C Scientists predicted that the earth would pass through the tail of the comet.

   D Newspapers ran stories about the dangers people faced.

2. **Which statement supports Marshall Applewhite's belief that an alien spaceship was coming?**

   F He believed Bonnie Lu was coming back.

   G Chuck Shramek went on TV to report a UFO in Hale-Bopp's tail.

   H Do expected the spaceship to take him and his followers to a new world.

   J He believed Hale-Bopp was a sign.

PERSUADE WITH AN EVIDENCE Write two sentences persuading your reader that an alien spaceship is following in Hale-Bopp's tail. The first sentence should summarize your story. The second sentence should try to prove that your story is true.

_____

_____

_____

_____

_____

SELECTION 1

Fowl Play at the Beach

60

Was it a threat or was it entertainment? On Sunday, August 19, 2001, something suddenly swooped down on a girl and two adults. Newspaper headlines described it with words such as "terrorizes" and "menacing." But many people found it rather amusing. For four days it attracted crowds of spectators as well as the media. They all gathered at Hampton Beach, New Hampshire. Almost everyone held a camera or a camcorder hoping to get a good shot of it. The "it" was a young eagle with a six-foot wingspan.

The eagle, it was later learned, had begun its adventures in North Carolina. It had been injured on May 17. It was then nursed back to health at the Carolina Raptor Center near Charlotte. On July 25, the eagle had recovered and was released back into the wild. Because it was a young bird, it had not yet established its own territory or taken a mate. It was free to roam wherever it chose. For three weeks, the eagle flew north. By the time it reached New Hampshire, it had covered about a thousand miles. Eric Aldrich, a wildlife expert, said, "It's not unusual for a young eagle to fly that far."

Unfortunately, the eagle must have had a lot of contact with people along the way. Perhaps it spent time with some fishermen. Perhaps it lingered with sunbathers along the coast. Or maybe it just remembered the kind people at the Carolina Raptor Center. In any case, by the time the eagle reached New Hampshire, it had lost its fear of humans.

On August 19, it made its appearance at Hampton Beach by buzzing beachgoers. It scratched one person on the ankles and picked at the legs of another. Then the eagle flew off, going from roof to roof along the buildings that lined the beach. Once in a while it returned to the beach to pick up a ball, a small football, or a bit of food.

Police and wildlife authorities were called to the beach. For the next few days, they tried to trap the eagle with food. They put dead fish inside a coiled wire cage. They even tried tossing dead fish and dead mice into the air. It was no use. The eagle wasn't hungry. People on the beach were leaving food out for it. They were luring it down so they could take photographs. "He associates people with food and that's the worst possible situation for a wild bird," said animal control officer Peter MacKinnon.

On August 21, things turned a bit more serious. That day the eagle clawed three-year-old Kayla Finn on the back. She was running down the beach with a football when the eagle flew down at her. Luckily, Kayla's father was nearby. He quickly pushed the eagle off Kayla. The little girl was scared but not hurt. "It was trying to play with me," she said. Perhaps that was true. Still, officials knew that next time the powerful bird might really hurt someone. And so they stepped up their efforts to capture it.

Officials tried going after the eagle while it was perched on various rooftops. But every time they got close, the eagle flew away. One man climbed to the roof of a three-story beach house and tried to snare the bird with a net. But the eagle was too quick. It flew off before the man could catch it.

The eagle clearly liked to snatch toy balls. So two officials stood on the beach, tossing a colorful little football back and forth. An animal control officer waited nearby with a net. But the eagle didn't take the bait. It just sat on the roof of the Ashworth Hotel, watching and waiting. It refused to budge.

Officials were worried that the eagle would hurt someone. But they were also worried that the eagle might hurt itself. Hampton Beach was no place for it. The area was much too crowded and noisy, and the streets had many overhead wires in which the eagle could get tangled up. In addition, some of the items found on the beach might prove harmful to it.

Finally, on August 22, the eagle left New Hampshire. It flew south to Salisbury Beach in Massachusetts. Once again, it attacked a child playing with a football. An eight-year-old boy suffered scratches on his back and collarbone.

Police were called to the scene. "When we arrived, the boy was being attended to by lifeguards," police officer Kevin Pike said. "The eagle was perched on the top of a three-story building facing the beach."

The police cleared the beach. Then Jim Lindley, an animal control officer, began tossing a tennis ball in the air. That caught the eagle's attention. It flew around in a circle and landed back on the roof. Lindley tossed the ball again. This time the eagle landed on the beach just a few feet away. Lindley took out some roast beef and ham he had brought along. "Jim lured the bird to him with the meat," said Pike, "then grabbed its talons and threw a blanket over it to keep it calm." The eagle, added Pike, "went quietly."

Just like that, it was over. The elusive eagle had been impossible to catch at Hampton Beach. But by the time it got to Salisbury Beach, it was hungry. And the key to this eagle's capture, it turned out, was its stomach.

If you have been timed while reading this article, enter your reading time below. Then turn to the Words-per-Minute Table on page 120 and look up your reading speed (words per minute). Enter your reading speed on the graph on page 121.

Reading Time: Selection 1

_____ : _____
MINUTES   SECONDS

UNDERSTANDING IDEAS
Circle the letter of the best answer.

1. **All of the following are theories about why the eagle wasn't afraid of humans EXCEPT**
   A it disliked human food
   B it may have spent time with some fishermen
   C it may have played with sunbathers on its way up the coast
   D it may have remembered the people at the Carolina Raptor Center

2. **Where did the eagle begin its adventure?**
   F Hampton Beach
   G Ashworth Hotel
   H Salisbury Beach
   J Carolina Raptor Center

3. **The eagle most likely attacked the little girl because it**
   A was hungry
   B wanted to play
   C was trying to kill her
   D wanted to scare her

4. **How was the eagle finally caught?**
   F with a net
   G with a colorful football
   H with roast beef and ham
   J with dead fish inside a cage

SUMMARIZE
For each blank, choose the word that best completes the meaning of the paragraph.

injured	buzzing	afraid
friends	coast	health

In August 2001, an eagle began

_____ beachgoers at Hampton

Beach in New Hampshire. As a young bird, the eagle had

been _____. It was nursed back

to _____ at the Carolina Raptor

Center in North Carolina. Once released, the eagle flew

up the _____. Along the way, it

apparently made some _____.

By the time it arrived in New Hampshire, it was no longer

_____ of people.

IF YOU WERE THERE
Pretend you are a wildlife authority called to Hampton Beach. Write a brief paragraph explaining how you would have tried to catch the eagle. Be sure to include examples from the story to support your response.

_____

_____

_____

_____

Moose on the Loose

Halloween costumes aren't really meant to scare anyone. They're just fun for children to wear when they go trick-or-treating. But no one explained that to the moose. In 2001, two children wearing Halloween costumes scared a moose while walking down a street in Anchorage, Alaska. The frightened animal charged nine-year-old Lydia Forbes and her six-year-old brother, Taylor.

The children, who were out walking with their dad, were lucky. They suffered only a few cuts and bruises. Still, it was a warning. A moose is usually a calm, slow-moving animal. But a scared moose can move with deadly speed. No one wants to be in front of a 1000-pound moose when it decides to charge.

In Anchorage, the local people know all about moose. These animals are a common sight. Moose will often wander into backyards looking for something to eat. So most Alaskans don't pay much attention when they see one. The abundance of moose was one reason why Kary Erickson moved to Alaska. "I couldn't imagine living anywhere else," she said after living there for seven years. "One of my favorite aspects of living here is having wildlife in my backyard."

But on November 29, 1994, Erickson learned how dangerous moose can be. Early that morning, she was out walking two dogs. On her way back home, she saw a cow moose with her calf. The creatures were in her neighbor's backyard across the street, nibbling on some shrubs. The dogs saw the moose, too, but didn't bark. The cow moose looked up and then returned to eating. Then, just as Erickson and the dogs were passing the moose, the calf suddenly got nervous.

Sensing danger, the cow moose charged toward the dogs. The dogs dashed away through the deep snow. The moose then turned toward Erickson, who was still standing on the street. Erickson did the best thing she could under the circumstances. She jumped into a snow bank. "I had nothing else nearby to protect me and no time to run anywhere."

As it turns out, lying flat with your hands around your head is one of the best things to do when a moose attacks. Rick Sinnott, a fish and game biologist, said, "As long as you are down on the ground, you are not a threat to the animal."

This moose, however, was really angry. She began to stomp on Erickson's feet, legs, and back. Erickson tried to protect her head and face. But the moose kept attacking. Finally, Erickson decided to play dead. She hoped that would make the moose go away. Said Erickson, "I remember hearing her breathing and I opened my eyes to see her standing within a couple of feet from my head. It was a very terrifying feeling."

At last, the moose lost interest. She moved away with her calf. But Erickson was left with deep bruises, three broken ribs, and a lacerated kidney. She believed the deep snow cushioned the blows and saved her life.

A deadly attack by a moose is rare. But it does happen. In 1999, a bull moose killed Brian Edwards of Montana. Edwards died from head injuries after the moose hit him with its antlers. It was the first fatal moose attack in southwestern Montana in twenty years. In Anchorage, moose killed two people during the 1990s. Experts say any moose can be dangerous. But two situations should always be avoided. Never get between a cow moose and her calf. And never get near a bull moose during the mating season. That is when the animals contend for the position of dominant male in the herd.

The greatest danger that moose pose to humans, however, is on the road. When a car strikes a deer, the deer usually dies and the car may be damaged. When a car strikes a moose, it's much worse. The average moose weighs ten times as much as the average deer. It is also much taller. When a car hits a deer, the grill takes the main blow. When a car hits a moose, however, the grill hits the animal's legs. The massive body of the moose hits the windshield.

Auto accidents involving moose are a particular problem in Maine. This state has a large moose herd. Moose often show up along the sides of roads. They like to lick the salt that has been spread to keep the road free of ice. Every year in Maine there are more than 600 moose-car accidents. Such accidents are almost always fatal for the moose. Sometimes they are fatal for the people, as well.

Like all wild animals, moose are best appreciated from a safe distance. As Kary Erickson said after her encounter with the cow moose, "I will be much more cautious about moose in the future, and I will do everything possible to detour around them."

If you have been timed while reading this article, enter your reading time below. Then turn to the Words-per-Minute Table on page 120 and look up your reading speed (words per minute). Enter your reading speed on the graph on page 121.

Reading Time: Selection 2

_____ : _____
MINUTES   SECONDS

UNDERSTANDING IDEAS Circle the letter of the best answer.

1. **Which statement belongs in the empty box?**

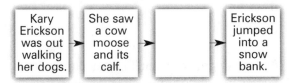

| Kary Erickson was out walking her dogs. | → | She saw a cow moose and its calf. | → | | → | Erickson jumped into a snow bank. |

   A Erickson reached out to pet the calf.

   B The dogs began to bark at the moose and calf.

   C The cow moose charged Erickson and her dogs.

   D The cow moose lost interest in Erickson.

2. **What is the best thing to do if a moose attacks you?**

   F Jump into a snow bank.

   G Run indoors as fast as you can.

   H Stand between the cow moose and her calf.

   J Lie flat with your hands around your head.

3. **Moose are often on the side of the road in Maine because**

   A they like to chase the cars that pass

   B it is easier for them to walk on the road

   C they like to lick the salt on the road

   D they eat the shrubs that grow near the road

4. **What will Kary Erickson most likely do the next time she meets a cow moose?**

   F call for help

   G avoid an encounter

   H give the moose some food

   J lie flat with hands around her head

SUMMARIZE For each blank, choose the word that best completes the meaning of the paragraph.

killed	cow	attack
Halloween	dangerous	common

   Moose are a _____ sight in states like Alaska and Montana. They can be extremely dangerous when they _____. Two children were attacked in 2001, when their _____ costumes scared a moose. Kary Erickson was attacked when a _____ moose was worried about her calf. In 1999, a bull moose _____ Brian Edwards. But moose are most _____ when hit by cars on the road.

IF YOU WERE THERE Write a brief paragraph explaining what you would do if you were attacked by a moose. Be sure to include examples from the story to support your response.

_____

_____

_____

_____

_____

_____

USE CONTEXT CLUES When you read, you may find a word whose meaning is unfamiliar to you. When that happens, you can look up the word's meaning in the dictionary. You can also find out what the word means by looking for context clues. These are words or sentences that come before or after the word. Context clues can be synonyms or antonyms of the unfamiliar word. They may also be an example or definition of the unfamiliar word.

Read each excerpt from the stories you just read. Circle the letter with the best meaning of the underlined word.

1. **But many people found it rather amusing. For four days it attracted crowds of <u>spectators</u> as well as the media.**

   A experts

   B onlookers

   C zookeepers

   D bird watchers

2. **Perhaps it spent time with some fishermen. Perhaps it <u>lingered</u> with sunbathers along the coast.**

   F attacked

   G escaped

   H stayed

   J enjoyed

3. **Most Alaskans don't pay much attention when they see one. The <u>abundance</u> of moose was one reason why Kary Erickson moved to Alaska.**

   A lack

   B breed

   C special coloring

   D large amount

4. **But Erickson was left with deep bruises, three broken ribs, and a <u>lacerated</u> kidney.**

   F torn

   G patched

   H useless

   J dangerous

5. **And never get near a bull moose during the mating season. That is when the animals contend for the position of <u>dominant</u> male in the herd.**

   A meanest

   B most powerful

   C tallest

   D most bashful

PUT WORDS INTO CONTEXT Complete the paragraph using the underlined words from the exercise on this page.

In Alaska, where there is an

_____ of moose, it is important

to stay alert. This is especially true during

mating season, when moose fight to become the

_____ male in the herd. Any

_____ could be seriously injured.

Those who have _____ around

agitated moose have sometimes come away with

bruises, _____ organs, or worse.

WORDS THAT COMPARE AND CONTRAST One type of context clue compares or contrasts an unfamiliar word to a familiar word or concept. When you see words and phrases such as *alike, different, both, also, in contrast, but,* and *yet,* you can tell that a comparison or contrast of an unfamiliar term will follow.

For numbers 1 through 8, read the complete paragraph. For each numbered blank, refer to the corresponding answer at the right. Choose the word that best completes the meaning of the paragraph.

The stories "Fowl Play at the Beach" and "Moose on the Loose" are (1)_____ because they

(2)_____ describe animal attacks.

(3)_____, the attacks they describe

are quite (4)_____. "Fowl Play

at the Beach" describes a playful eagle.

(5)_____, "Moose on the Loose"

recounts several serious moose attacks.

(6)_____ eagles and moose can

(7)_____ cause serious injuries to

humans, it is (8)_____ that moose

attacks are usually more deadly.

1. **A** likewise
   B identical
   C relative
   D similar

2. **F** also
   G same
   H both
   J equal

3. **A** Similarly
   B Likewise
   C However
   D Either

4. **F** another
   G different
   H separate
   J unlike

5. **A** although
   B in contrast
   C furthermore
   D in addition

6. **F** while
   G however
   H on one hand
   J in other ways

7. **A** neither
   B each
   C too
   D either

8. **F** disagree
   G likely
   H contrast
   J distinct

ORGANIZE THE FACTS The two stories you read in this unit are alike in some ways and different in other ways. A Venn diagram can show how they are alike and different. Look at the Venn diagram below. Then choose the best answer to each question.

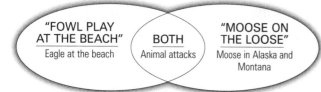

"FOWL PLAY AT THE BEACH"
Eagle at the beach

BOTH
Animal attacks

"MOOSE ON THE LOOSE"
Moose in Alaska and Montana

1. **Which of the following details belongs in the oval marked "BOTH"?**

   A The animal causes only minor injuries.

   B The animal has lost its fear of humans.

   C The animal is scared by Halloween costumes.

   D The animal could possibly hurt someone very badly.

2. **Which detail does NOT belong in the oval marked "Fowl Play at the Beach"?**

   F The animal can be lured by roast beef and ham.

   G The animal likes to play with colorful footballs.

   H The animal enjoys licking salt from the road.

   J The animal associates people with food.

3. **Which detail does NOT belong in the oval marked "Moose on the Loose"?**

   A Never approach the animal during mating season.

   B The animal should be captured as soon as possible.

   C The animal attacks when it is protecting its young.

   D The animal can destroy a car if hit on the road.

4. **Which detail does NOT belong in either story?**

   F The animal hasn't established a territory yet.

   G The animal often wanders into backyards.

   H The animal could get tangled in overhead wires.

   J The animal swims for hours to catch its prey.

CONTINUE THE COMPARISON Fill in the chart with four additional details about how the stories are alike. Then fill in the chart on the bottom with four additional details about how the stories are different.

More ways the stories are alike:

More ways the stories are different:

MAKE INFERENCES An author doesn't always state an idea directly in a passage. You can often determine what the idea is by applying your own knowledge and experience or by examining the evidence presented in the text. This is called making an inference. Circle the letter of the best answer.

1. **What can the reader infer from the following sentences?**

> Such accidents are almost always fatal for the moose. Some are fatal for people as well.

   A People always die in car accidents with moose.

   B People can die in car accidents with moose.

   C No one ever dies in a car accident with a moose.

   D People do not get into car accidents with moose.

2. **What can the reader infer from the first sentence of the story?**

> "Halloween costumes aren't really meant to scare anyone."

   F Halloween costumes are never scary.

   G A moose charges a girl and her brother.

   H Something is scared by the Halloween costumes.

   J Two children dressed up like a moose for Halloween.

3. **What is the best inference a reader can make about this sentence?**

> So most Alaskans don't pay much attention when they see [a moose].

   A Alaskans pay extra attention to all the moose.

   B Alaskans don't ever notice moose.

   C There are too many moose in Alaska.

   D Moose are a common sight in Alaska.

APPLY WHAT YOU KNOW Choose the best answer.

1. **What do you think the author intended to do in the first paragraph of "Fowl Play at the Beach"?**

   A make the reader curious

   B compare two different events

   C write a history of Hampton Beach

   D explain how an eagle eats

2. **By saying "It was not unusual for a young eagle to fly that far," the author probably wanted to**

   F present the eagle as terrorizing and menacing

   G show that this detail of the story is more believable

   H convince the reader that the eagle is special

   J inform readers that the eagle is not like other eagles

JUDGE THE EVIDENCE Based on what you have read in both stories, do you think wild animals are a menace or simply misunderstood? Write a brief paragraph stating your opinion. Support your position with evidence from the stories you have read.

_____

_____

_____

_____

_____

_____

Big Rocks, Little Rocks

Doomsday Rock

How old will you be in 2028? Or, more precisely, how old will you be on October 26, 2028? In 1998, astronomer Brian Marsden announced that this just might be the day when you and a lot of other people die. Marsden predicted that on this day a mile-wide asteroid called XF 11 might pass within 30,000 miles of the earth. He said it would happen at about 1:30 P.M. Eastern Daylight Time. Thirty thousand miles might sound like a long distance. But when you're dealing with outer space, it really isn't. The moon is 240,000 miles from the earth. So this would be much closer. Marsden even hinted that the asteroid could hit our planet.

The news triggered real fear among astronomers. "It scares me," said Jack Hills. "It really does." Hills worked at the Los Alamos National Laboratory. He knew what an asteroid that size would do if it landed on the earth.

Asteroids are large rocks that circle the sun. Scientists believe they are debris left over from the time when the solar system was born. Every once in a while, one of these asteroids hits the earth. The results can be catastrophic. Many scientists think that an asteroid killed the dinosaurs. Around 65 million years ago, a five-mile-wide asteroid landed in Mexico. It threw billions of tons of rock and dirt high up into the air. As the rocks fell back to the earth, they heated up. Their heat set off fires around the world. After the fires died out, the earth turned bitterly cold. The thick cloud of dirt caused by the asteroid blocked out the sun. No plants could grow. So the dinosaurs either froze to death or starved to death. One scientist remarked that the mystery wasn't how the dinosaurs died; it was how *anything* survived.

More recently, an asteroid fell in Siberia. This happened in 1908. Scientists think it exploded before hitting the ground. This asteroid was only two hundred feet wide. But the force of the blast flattened every tree within hundreds of square miles. It also killed all the deer and started major fires. Luckily, few people lived in the region. But the blast itself was so loud that it was heard thousands of miles away in London.

Is Asteroid XF 11 a doomsday rock? It is not as big as the one that wiped out the dinosaurs. But it is a lot bigger than the one that hit Siberia. It would strike the earth at a speed of about 38,000 miles an hour. The combination of size and speed would give it a terrific wallop. If it landed in the ocean, it would send waves around the world. The waves would be hundreds of feet high. They would wipe out coastal cities. "Where cities stood," said Hills, "there would be mudflats."

If XF 11 hit land, it would cause a blast equal to that of a 300,000-megaton bomb. That is twenty million times more powerful than the atomic bomb that leveled the city of Hiroshima! If it struck near a city, millions of people would die in a flash. Even if it landed in a remote place, it would spell disaster. The blast would create a crater thirty miles wide. It would send huge amounts of dirt and ash into the air. The dust would block out the sun for months. Without sunlight, crops could not grow. Millions of people would starve to death. Those who lived would face harsh conditions on a devastated planet.

So it was no wonder that Hills and other astronomers were a little edgy when they heard Marsden's prediction. They began to check their records and old photos. One of these astronomers was Eleanor Helin. She worked for the Near Earth Asteroid Tracking (NEAT) program. Helin pulled out some photographs taken in 1990. The asteroid was there, but no one had noticed it before. These photos proved to be very important. Marsden's prediction was based on data for just three months. Now, with Helin's photographs, astronomers could look at the asteroid's movement over eight years. They could

plot its future path much more accurately. After checking the new data, astronomers breathed a huge sigh of relief. XF 11 would miss the earth by about six hundred thousand miles. There was really no chance that it would strike the earth.

Of course, there are other asteroids out there. Scientists have found two hundred that cross the earth's orbit. There might be as many as two thousand more. Will one of these be the doomsday rock? Most scientists think so. Over the years, our planet has been struck by hundreds of asteroids. It will get hit again. There's no "maybe" about it; the only question is "when"?

Still, you don't need to lose sleep over it. Scientists already have ideas on how to blow up or divert an asteroid that is heading toward the earth. Even when he thought XF 11 might hit the earth, Marsden stayed calm. "If it was only a few months away, we should be deadly worried," he said. "But with 30 years, astronomers will solve the problem." Luckily, in this particular case they won't have to.

If you have been timed while reading this article, enter your reading time below. Then turn to the Words-per-Minute Table on page 120 and look up your reading speed (words per minute). Enter your reading speed on the graph on page 121.

Reading Time: Selection 1

_____ : _____
MINUTES   SECONDS

UNDERSTANDING IDEAS Circle the letter of the best answer.

1. What news triggered fear among astronomers?

A An asteroid killed the dinosaurs.

B An asteroid landed in Siberia.

C The moon is 240,000 miles from the earth.

D XF 11 might pass within 30,000 miles of the earth.

2. Which theory about dinosaurs do many scientists believe?

F The earth became too hot for them.

G The dinosaurs blocked out the sun.

H They were killed when an asteroid hit the earth.

J The heat from dinosaurs set off fires.

3. What might happen if Asteroid XF 11 hit the earth?

A Crops could not grow.

B People would starve to death.

C Waves could wipe out coastal cities.

D all of the above

4. Why are scientists less worried about asteroids hitting the earth?

F They think Brian Marsden's warning is not based on fact.

G They have ideas on how to divert an asteroid.

H Asteroids circle the sun, not the planet Earth.

J Photographs show that asteroids are harmless.

SUMMARIZE For each blank, choose the word that best completes the meaning of the paragraph.

blocked	grow	
		scientists
asteroid	world	

In the past, when asteroids hit the earth, they set off fires around the _____. The thick cloud of dirt caused by an asteroid _____ the sun. Without the sun, no plants could _____ and everything froze. Some _____ believe that dinosaurs were wiped out after a five-mile-wide asteroid hit the earth. Today scientists believe they can figure out how to divert an _____ that comes too close to the earth.

IF YOU WERE THERE Write a brief paragraph explaining what you would do if you were tracking an asteroid and realized it was coming toward the earth. Be sure to include examples from the story to support your response.

_____

_____

_____

_____

_____

Cool Cash for a Hot Rock

On March 22, 1998, nine-year-old Flavio Armendariz was playing basketball in the driveway of his home in Monahans, Texas. Six of his friends were with him. Suddenly Flavio heard a very strange noise.

"I heard this boom-boom-boom sound," he said later.

Eleven-year-old Alvaro Lyles was about to shoot a three-pointer. But he, too, heard the loud sound. He tossed the basketball aside and looked over at the vacant lot next door. The sound seemed to have come from there.

Alvaro and Flavio rushed to the vacant lot to investigate. Flavio's brother, Neri, raced after them. So did the other boys—Patrick Lyles, José Falen, Eron Hernandez, and Javier Juarez. Flavio was the first one to reach the strange object embedded in the dirt. It turned out to be a 2-pound, 11-ounce black meteorite shaped like a peanut. The rock had fallen from outer space. "It was still warm," Flavio later recalled.

Meteorites are pieces of rock from outer space. They have broken off from comets or asteroids. Most of the time the pieces are tiny specks no bigger than a grain of sand. These tiny rocks plunge through the earth's atmosphere. A meteorite weighing over two pounds is rare.

When a large meteorite hits the earth, the media usually report it. On October 9, 1992, for example, a 30-pound meteorite hit a parked car in Peekskill, New York. It went right through the roof. It went through the floorboard, too. It left a small crater in the ground beneath the car. Fortunately, no one was in the car at the time. On December 10, 1992, a 15-pound meteorite hit a house in Japan. It crashed through the roof and the floor of the second story. Again, no one was hurt. In fact, there has never been a documented case of anyone being killed by a direct hit from a meteorite. But there was a 1997 incident in Colombia in which a meteorite hit a home and started a fire. Four children died in the blaze.

Flavio and his friends—soon called the Meteorite Seven—showed the rock to Orlando Lyles, the father of Alvaro and Patrick. He was an amateur astronomer. Right away he knew that the rock was a meteorite. He also knew that the find was newsworthy. "We thought it would be neat to get media attention," he said.

Orlando reported the news to a local radio station. It didn't take long for hundreds of people to flock to the vacant lot. They wanted to see the rock. Firefighters also came. They thought the meteorite might be radioactive. So they took it from the boys. They promised to return it as soon as NASA scientists at the LBJ Space Center near Houston said it was safe.

Orlando and the boys weren't happy about losing the rock, even for a short time. But there wasn't much they could do about it. "What was I supposed to do," lamented Orlando, "shoot 'em to keep 'em from taking it?"

It turned out that the meteorite was safe. But it was also valuable. It was worth thousands of dollars to people who collect such things. Monahans city officials didn't want to give it back to the Meteorite Seven. When the boys asked for it, the mayor of Monahans refused. He sent the boys a letter pointing out that the meteorite had landed on public property. Therefore, he said, it belonged to the city. The city manager agreed with the mayor. He said the meteorite was the "property of the citizens of Monahans."

The boys couldn't believe it. In their minds, the rock clearly belonged to them. After all, they reasoned, "finders, keepers."

At first, it appeared that the city would dig in its heels and fight for the rock. But it soon became clear that almost everyone in Monahans backed the boys. On June 9, the city council held a meeting. The public gallery was packed. As people watched, the council voted 4 to 0 to let the boys keep the meteorite.

"I'm very excited," said Alvaro Lyles. "We won, and now it's ours. It's cool that they didn't try to trick us out of what was ours."

Orlando Lyles pointed out that the boys "learned a worthwhile lesson. If you're right, you can fight city hall and win."

In July, the Meteorite Seven put the rock up for auction. Mike Craddock, a rare rock collector and businessman, made the highest bid. He paid $23,000 to become the rock's new owner. The boys split the money equally. They used some to buy bikes and video games. But they saved most of the money for college.

Ultimately, the money wasn't the most important thing to the boys. It was the thrill of finding something so rare. "If they had wound up with $10 apiece, they would have been happy," said Orlando. "That's the beauty of being a kid."

If you have been timed while reading this article, enter your reading time below. Then turn to the Words-per-Minute Table on page 120 and look up your reading speed (words per minute). Enter your reading speed on the graph on page 121.

Reading Time: Selection 2

_____ : _____
MINUTES   SECONDS

UNDERSTANDING IDEAS Circle the letter of the best answer.

1. **Why did the Meteorite Seven rush to the vacant lot?**

   A They found a warm rock.

   B The ball bounced into the lot.

   C They wanted to play basketball.

   D They heard a very strange noise.

2. **What was unique about the meteorite that they found?**

   F It was radioactive.

   G It was shaped like a peanut.

   H It weighed over two pounds.

   J It looked like a shooting star.

3. **Which was the most convincing reason for taking the rock away from the boys who found it?**

   A The meteorite might be radioactive.

   B The rock was very valuable to collectors.

   C Anything from outer space belongs to NASA.

   D Hundreds of other people in the vacant lot saw the meteorite fall, too.

4. **The city council probably voted in favor of the boys because**

   F the meteorite had landed on public property

   G almost everyone agreed that finders should be keepers

   H the boys agreed to share the money with the citizens of Monahan

   J they decided to fight city hall

SUMMARIZE For each blank, choose the word that best completes the meaning of the paragraph.

valuable	meteorite	
		weighed
case	harmless	

Seven boys found a peanut-shaped rock that

_____ over two pounds. They

showed the rock to an amateur astronomer who knew right

away that it was a _____.

NASA scientists studied the meteorite and found it to be

_____. Instead of returning the rock

to the boys, the city council decided that it was

_____ city property. With most of

the citizens backing them up, the boys won the

_____ and sold the rock to

a collector.

IF YOU WERE THERE Write a brief paragraph explaining what you would do if you found a meteorite. Where would you take it? Be sure to include examples from the story to support your response.

_____

_____

_____

_____

_____

USE CONTEXT CLUES When you read, you may find a word whose meaning is unfamiliar to you. When that happens, you can look up the word's meaning in the dictionary. You can also find out what the word means by looking for context clues. These are words or sentences that come before or after the word. Context clues can be synonyms or antonyms of the unfamiliar word. They may also be an example or definition of the unfamiliar word.

Read each excerpt from the stories you just read. Circle the letter with the best meaning of the underlined word.

1. **Thirty thousand miles might sound like a long <u>distance</u>. But when you're dealing with outer space, it really isn't.**

   A avoiding to meet

   B calling from far away

   C the space between two places

   D the ability to drive

2. **Every once in a while, one of these asteroids hits the earth. The results can be <u>catastrophic</u>. Many scientists think that an asteroid killed the dinosaurs.**

   F unavoidable

   G relaxing

   H fast and quick

   J the cause of a terrible disaster

3. **Scientists already have ideas on how to blow up or <u>divert</u> an asteroid that is heading toward the earth.**

   A cause to take a different route

   B burn into small pieces

   C direct toward a planned target

   D lose track of where it should be

4. **When a large meteorite hits the earth, the media usually report it. . . . In fact, there has never been a <u>documented</u> case of anyone being killed by a direct hit from a meteorite.**

   F different

   G recorded

   H surprised

   J unknown

5. **At first, it appeared that the city would <u>dig in its heels</u> and fight for the rock. But it soon became clear that almost everyone in Monahans backed the boys.**

   A give in

   B be very firm

   C rule out

   D search

PUT WORDS INTO CONTEXT Complete the paragraph using the underlined words from the exercise on this page.

There have been several _____

events caused by asteroids. Some of these events were

_____ by scientists. They track

asteroids even if their distance from the earth is millions of

miles away. They want to be sure there is always a big

_____ between asteroids

and the earth.

MAKE ROOT CONNECTIONS One way of finding out the meaning of a word is by looking for its root. An unfamiliar word may share a common root with a word that you know. A root is a part of many different words and may not be a word by itself. The root *aster* or *astro* comes from a Greek word that means "star." You will find the root in words like *asteroid* and *astronomy*.

Underline the root that connects each group of words. Then choose the best meaning of the root.

1. **document, docudrama, documentary**
   A based on real events
   B roles taken by actors
   C made of paper and ink
   D stories made from imagination

2. **predict, dictation, verdict**
   F to lie
   G to say
   H to recall
   J to foresee

3. **scientists, conscience, scientific**
   A to believe
   B to know
   C to make
   D to search

4. **investigate, vestige, investigator**
   F track or trace
   G touch or feel
   H hint or tell
   J invest or earn

5. **vacant, evacuate, vacuum**
   A hidden
   B lock
   C empty
   D invade

6. **valuable, invalid, valor**
   F to be cold
   G to have worth
   H to show bravery
   J to move quickly

ROOT ANALOGIES Analogies show similar patterns and relationships between words. Root analogies show relationships between words that have the same root word. For example, *use* is to *useable* as *move* is to *moveable*. Both root words, when combined with *able*, make a new word. For each blank, choose one of the boldfaced words from the exercise on this page to correctly complete the analogy.

1. *pend* is to *pendant* as *vac* is to

   _____ .

2. *dur* is to *durable* as *val* is to

   _____ .

3. *bea* is to *beatific* as *scien* is to

   _____ .

4. *contra* is to *contradict* as *pre* is to

   _____ .

5. *element* is to *elementary* as *document* is to

   _____ .

FIND THE PURPOSE Authors write to inform or teach, to persuade or convince, or to entertain. Many times authors write for more than one purpose. Advertisements, for example, can fit all three purposes for writing. The ad may inform you about a product or service you can buy. It attempts to persuade you to buy it, and it may be entertaining so that it appeals readily to a large number of people.

Read the chart below. Then answer the questions.

Author's Purpose		
to inform (teach)	**to persuade (convince)**	**to entertain (amuse)**
• teach history, science, and other subjects	• argue for or against an issue	• appeal to a reader's interest
• report an event	• to convince people to buy	• make people laugh
• explain a process	• tell people how to act	• tell a personal story
• describe facts	• offer the best solution to a problem	• put words together in a poem

1. **If a scientist wrote an article explaining where a meteorite comes from, what would be the primary purpose of the article?**

   A to inform

   B to persuade

   C to entertain

   D all of the above

2. **What would be the purpose of a humorous movie about the Meteorite Seven?**

   F to inform

   G to persuade

   H to entertain

   J all of the above

3. **What was the purpose of the letter written by the mayor of Monahans to the Meteorite Seven?**

   A to inform

   B to persuade

   C to entertain

   D all of the above

4. **The writer of a humorous play designed to promote more studies about how dinosaurs vanished would have what purpose?**

   F to inform

   G to persuade

   H to entertain

   J all of the above

WRITE WITH A PURPOSE Write a topic sentence about asteroids or meteorites for each of the purposes you reviewed in this lesson.

to inform: _____

_____

to persuade: _____

_____

to entertain: _____

_____

MAKE PREDICTIONS You can make predictions, or educated guesses, based on what you already know. For instance, if you know that collectors buy rare rocks, you can reasonably predict that they would buy a unique meteorite.

Read this passage, and answer the following questions based on what you know after reading the stories in this unit.

Close Encounter

NASA astronomers continue to refine the ways they analyze potential hazards from space. Recently, they discovered an asteroid that is two-thirds of a mile wide. They named it 1950 DA. Studying its orbital path, the scientists predict that the asteroid will come close to the earth on March 16, 2880. Based on what is known so far, odds for a collision with the earth are now 1 in 300. But the odds could change.

---

1. **What do you predict people would feel if scientists announced that the asteroid would hit the earth very soon?**

   A anger

   B fear

   C pain

   D relaxed

2. **Based on what you know about scientific methods, what do you predict the astronomers would do next?**

   F go to the asteroid for a closer look

   G discover other asteroids in the same orbit

   H ignore the asteroid

   J develop more advanced ways of predicting the asteroid's route

3. **Suppose the odds for a collision change to one in five. What do you predict scientists will do?**

   A invent ways to redirect the asteroid

   B declare the asteroid harmless

   C describe what might happen

   D tell people to evacuate their homes

JUDGE THE BASIS OF A PREDICTION For predictions to be reasonably accurate, they must be based on what you know as factual information. Choose the best answer.

1. **Which information helps you predict that scientists will identify any asteroid that can potentially destroy the earth?**

   A Scientists are paying less attention to asteroids than they used to.

   B They discovered an asteroid two-thirds of a mile wide.

   C Scientists are able to identify hazards 800 years into the future as well as today.

   D Odds for a collision with the earth are 1 in 300.

2. **Which information would help you predict that large asteroids will no longer land on the earth?**

   F NASA reports the discovery of the largest asteroid.

   G Radar has identified an asteroid near the moon.

   H Scientists have discovered better ways of photographing asteroids.

   J A new weapon has been built to destroy oncoming asteroids.

PREDICT WHAT YOU WOULD DO Write a brief paragraph explaining what you predict might happen if a large rock fell in your backyard. Use examples from the stories you have just read to explain your actions.

_____

_____

_____

_____

_____

_____

_____

SELECTION 1

No Margin for Error

"It's the closest you're ever going to get to being a bird," says Stewart Karstens, a pilot from New Zealand.

Karstens doesn't fly a real plane. Instead, he's a paraglider pilot. His "aircraft" weighs just 15 pounds and can be carried in a backpack. Like a parachute, it has a nylon chute with a few lines that connect it to a small harness. Like a hang glider, it allows people to take off from the ground. One writer described the banana-shaped paraglider as little more than a "designer handkerchief."

According to experts such as Karstens, paragliding is a very safe sport *if* you follow certain rules. "If your equipment is not up to snuff," said Joachim Lang, a paragliding teacher, "it's your fault because you haven't checked it out." If you go out and the winds are bad, it's your fault because you should have checked them out first. And if you make a mistake while flying, well, it's your fault again. Paragliders fly thousands of feet above the ground. One mistake can send you crashing to your death. In paragliding there is no margin for error.

Onno Bertsma learned that the hard way. On May 14, 2001, this Dutch tourist was making his second flight of the day from the summit of Port Hills in New Zealand. Just as he was about to land, his chute became tangled in some high-tension power lines. Luckily, the crash tripped a safety wire. That cut off the power in the lines. "It's lucky he did not fry himself on the power lines," said rescuer Evan Roper.

Still, Bertsma was caught high above the ground. The ground under the power lines was too steep for a land-based rescue. Rescuers had to call in a helicopter for help. That almost led to disaster because the wind created by the helicopter blades caused the parachute to start filling up with air. Bertsma spun around and, for a brief moment, it looked as if the chute would break free and send him plummeting to the ground. The chopper backed off and waited until Bertsma freed himself from his chute. Then a rescuer was lowered from the helicopter on a wire. As the rescuer dangled from the wire, he was able to grab Bertsma and carry him to safety.

Bertsma was luckier than Andrew Stephen. On March 25, 2000, Stephen was paragliding in Nelson, New Zealand. Stewart Karstens was his instructor. Stephen had already flown forty times and was working to get his intermediate pilot rating. During his previous flights, he had flown an older model paraglider. This time he decided to try a newer one.

Karstens always warns his students not to do anything they don't feel comfortable doing. Lydie Guyot, Stephen's girlfriend, later said Stephen was a bit nervous about using the new glider. "I remember him telling me he just wasn't feeling secure about it," Guyot said.

On the way to the launch site, Stephen talked to Karstens about his fears. They talked about wind currents, air traffic, and the new equipment. Once more Karstens cautioned him not to do anything that made him feel uncomfortable. Whatever Karstens said must have eased Stephen's mind because he decided to make the flight.

In the beginning, Stephen soared like an eagle. "I saw him flying. He was having a great time, he seemed to be loving it," remembered Guyot, who had gone part way down the mountain to take pictures. "He was making great turns and taking advantage of the thermals."

Guyot took her eyes off Stephen for a moment. When she looked up again, she saw him spiraling out of control toward the ground. His parachute was at a 90-degree angle to the ground. Something had gone tragically wrong.

Next Guyot heard the siren of an ambulance. She just sat on the mountain for 45 minutes, afraid to move. Then someone came to get her. At the bottom of the mountain, she saw paramedics working on Stephen. "When we arrived at the landing ground they tried to keep me away from him," said Guyot. "No one talked to me . . . I'm sure they knew [he was dead]; they were all looking at me."

At last, two police officers walked over and gave her the bad news. "I felt like it wasn't real," she said.

But, of course, it was. Somehow Andrew Stephen had turned the wrong way and put his glider into a steep vertical dive. He hadn't been able to pull out of it. He made that one mistake, and he paid for it with his life.

If you have been timed while reading this article, enter your reading time below. Then turn to the Words-per-Minute Table on page 120 and look up your reading speed (words per minute). Enter your reading speed on the graph on page 121.

Reading Time: Selection 1

—————— : ——————
MINUTES   SECONDS

UNDERSTANDING IDEAS Circle the letter of the best answer.

1. **A paraglider most looks like**

   A a designer handkerchief

   B a bird with large wings

   C a hot air balloon

   D a small airplane

2. **How can a paraglider ensure safety?**

   F fly only when the winds are strong

   G follow the rules and not make mistakes

   H learn paragliding skills the hard way

   J fly thousands of feet above the ground

3. **Why was Onno Bertsma luckier than Andrew Stephen?**

   A Onno survived the crash; Andrew didn't.

   B Onno's paraglider was safer than Andrew's.

   C Onno flew in May; Andrew flew in March.

   D Onno felt more comfortable about the flight.

4. **Based on the incidents in the story, which conclusion can a reader draw about paragliding?**

   F All paragliders are crazy.

   G Only expert pilots should fly.

   H Paragliding can be very dangerous.

   J Flying a paraglider must be a lot of fun.

SUMMARIZE For each blank, choose the word that best completes the meaning of the paragraph.

favorable	check	mistakes
death	rules	tangled

Paragliding is a sport that does not allow any

_____. Paragliders can get seriously

hurt, even die, if they do not _____

their aircraft before every flight. They should also make

sure the winds are _____ before

they fly. One false move caused Onno Bertsma to

get_____ in power lines.

A wrong turn caused Andrew Stephen's

_____. However, some experts like

Stewart Karstens claim that the sport is safe if pilots

follow all the _____.

IF YOU WERE THERE Write a brief paragraph explaining what you would do if your best friend decided to go paragliding. Be sure to include examples from the story to support your response.

_____

_____

_____

_____

_____

The Fan Man

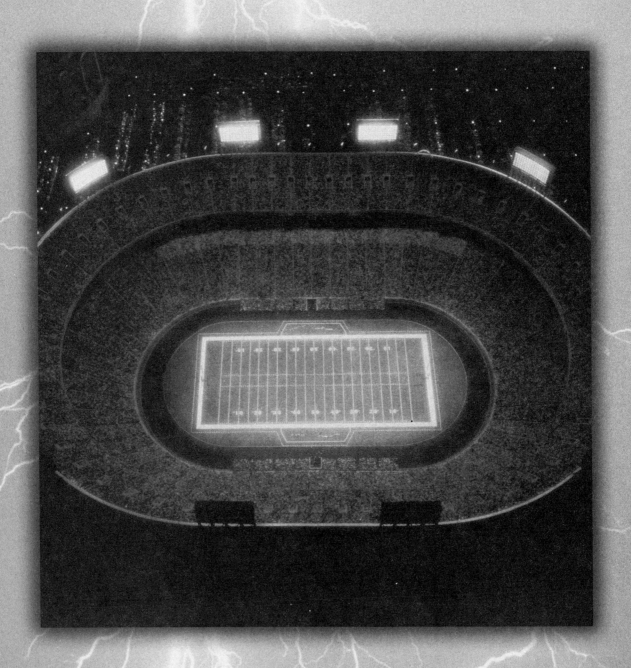

He called himself the "Fan Man." But sportswriter Wallace Matthews called him an Unidentified Flying Idiot, or "UFI." On November 6, 1993, James Miller took off in his paraglider. He headed for an outdoor arena behind Caesar's Palace in Las Vegas. Miller planned to drop from the sky and land in a boxing ring set up there. This was an odd plan at best. But what made it even stranger was that the Fan Man would be landing in the ring in the middle of a heavyweight championship fight!

The crowds who flocked to the arena that night had no knowledge of Miller's plan. Neither did the boxers, Riddick Bowe and Evander Holyfield. In fact, no one knew what Miller was planning to do. For the first six rounds of the fight, everything went smoothly. Bowe and Holyfield were waging an epic battle to see who would hold the world heavyweight title. Then Miller appeared in the sky. A police helicopter spotted him and warned him away. But Miller paid no attention. Instead, he aimed his fan-powered contraption toward the ring and began plunging downward. At one minute and ten seconds into the seventh round, he crashed feet-first into the ropes of the ring.

Holyfield and Bowe didn't know what was happening. "I didn't know what he was going to do, attack me or Bowe," said Holyfield. "But I tried to get out of the way. I was afraid he might have a gun or a bomb." Bowe's pregnant wife, Judy, was so stunned that she fainted and had to be rushed to the hospital. Luckily, both she and her baby were unharmed.

Bowe's ringside assistants were furious about the unexpected delay in the fight. Their man had been gaining momentum. They thought he had been about to win. Several of them grabbed Miller and began punching him. Security guards rushed in to restore order, but it took twenty minutes. At last, Miller was carried out of the arena on a stretcher. He wasn't hurt— but he could have been. He also could have injured the fighters or spectators. The county commissioner Thalia Dondero said, "He could have decapitated people there, the way he came in."

Although the fight eventually resumed, many people felt Miller's stunt ruined it. Wallace Matthews wrote that it turned the fight into a "freak show." He went on to add, "By the time they cleared away the debris and carted off the wounded, much of the juice had gone out of the bout."

The Fan Man was charged with flying an aircraft in a reckless manner. Later, the charge was changed to trespassing. Miller, a 30-year-old computer repairman from Nevada, didn't seem to care. He appeared in court wearing a crash helmet. When the judge ordered him to take it off, he complied—showing everyone his painted head. Miller pleaded guilty and served ten days in jail. He was banned from Caesar's Palace forever.

Two months later, Miller was back doing flying stunts. This time he flew his paraglider over the Los Angeles Coliseum during a football game. The L.A. Raiders were playing the Denver Broncos at the time. Once again, Miller's antics caused a commotion. The game was delayed for two minutes in the first quarter while everyone waited to see if he would try to land on the field. He didn't. Instead, he waved and dipped his wings several times, then went on to land in a nearby field. Police quickly arrested him. This time they charged him with interfering with a sporting event.

Shortly after that, Miller struck in London, England. He targeted Buckingham Palace, where the Queen lives. At 7:31 A.M. on February 5, 1994, Miller landed his paraglider right on the palace roof. As startled tourists watched, he took off his pants. He was painted green from the waist down. "Come and get me!" he shouted to the palace guards. Dozens of them did just that, and once again Miller was hauled off to jail.

This time Miller was charged with disrupting the public order and with violating five aviation rules. Again, Miller pleaded guilty. The judge fined him $293 and recommended he be deported. He was lucky to get off this lightly. Neither the Queen nor any other members of the royal family had been home when Miller landed on the roof. If they had been there, one source said, palace guards would have shot him.

No one was really sure why Miller was doing these wild things. Some thought he loved the publicity. Others thought he was hoping to get rich by selling stories of his exploits. Other people, however, had a simpler explanation. They concluded that the Fan Man was just plain nuts.

If you have been timed while reading this article, enter your reading time below. Then turn to the Words-per-Minute Table on page 120 and look up your reading speed (words per minute). Enter your reading speed on the graph on page 121.

Reading Time: Selection 2

_____ : _____
MINUTES   SECONDS

UNDERSTANDING IDEAS Circle the letter of the best answer.

1. **What was James Miller's plan in Las Vegas?**

   A swoop down, tip his wings, and land next door

   B land in the boxing ring during a championship bout

   C be in the middle of a fight so that he could write about it

   D call attention to his unusual machine and landing skills

2. **Which word BEST describes the athletes' reaction after Miller landed in the middle of a fight or game?**

   F amused

   G confused

   H relieved

   J embarrassed

3. **Where would the Fan Man most likely land next?**

   A in another ring at Caesar's Palace

   B in a stadium during a baseball game

   C where he can avoid being arrested

   D where he would get the most attention

4. **Based on what happened to Miller after every paragliding feat, which prediction could you make about his next flight?**

   F He will be injured.

   G He will stop flying.

   H He will be arrested.

   J He will write a story.

SUMMARIZE For each blank, choose the word that best completes the meaning of the paragraph.

fight	loves	chooses
punished	landed	game

A paraglider named James Miller

_____ the most unusual places to land.

He has crashed feet-first in the middle of a boxing ring

during a _____. He has swooped down

over a football field while a _____ was

going on. He has even _____ on the

roof of Buckingham Palace. In each case, Miller was

_____ for his actions. It seems,

however, that Miller does not care. He just

_____ to do these wild antics.

IF YOU WERE THERE Write a brief paragraph explaining what you would do if you met James Miller. Be sure to include examples from the story to support your response.

_____

_____

_____

_____

_____

_____

_____

USE CONTEXT CLUES When you read, you may find a word whose meaning is unfamiliar to you. When that happens, you can look up the word's meaning in the dictionary. You can also find out what the word means by looking for context clues. These are words or sentences that come before or after the word. Context clues can be synonyms or antonyms of the unfamiliar word. They may also be an example or definition of the unfamiliar word.

Read each excerpt from the stories you just read. Circle the letter with the best meaning of the underlined word.

1. **"If your equipment is not up to snuff," said Joachim Lang, a paragliding teacher, "it's your fault because you haven't checked it out."**

    A up in the air

    B in working order

    C running like a machine

    D making a puffing sound

2. **One mistake can send you crashing to your death. In paragliding there is no margin for error.**

    F harm as a result

    G danger in the sky

    H room for mistakes

    J report of accidents

3. **When she looked up again, she saw him spiraling out of control toward the ground. His parachute was at a 90-degree angle to the ground. Something had gone tragically wrong.**

    A forward

    B downward

    C seriously

    D wildly

4. **For the first six rounds of the fight, everything went smoothly. Bowe and Holyfield were waging an epic battle to see who would hold the world heavyweight title.**

    F a small argument

    G an incredible fight

    H a heated discussion

    J a sporting event

5. **No one was really sure why Miller was doing these wild things. . . . They concluded that the Fan Man was just plain nuts.**

    A very crazy

    B fond of nuts

    C simple and clear

    D looking for attention

PUT WORDS INTO CONTEXT Complete the paragraph using the underlined words from the exercise on this page.

Most people think that any person who takes up

paragliding is just _____ .

It is even crazier to land in a boxing ring during

_____ . Imagine if the Fan Man's

aircraft was not _____ . He could have

spiraled _____ toward the crowd

and hurt someone.

USING EXACT WORDS Exact words help to create a mental picture in the mind of the reader. For example, which sentence gives you a clearer image? (1) She saw him go down fast. (2) She saw him spiraling out of control toward the ground. Unlike Sentence 1, which creates only a general image, sentence 2 gives the reader a specific mental picture because it uses vivid verbs and descriptive words.

Read these sentences and choose the MOST exact descriptive phrase to replace the underlined words.

1. **One mistake can <u>hurt you</u>.**
   A kill you
   B cause injury
   C make you turn the wrong way
   D send you crashing to your death

2. **The ground under the power lines <u>made rescue impossible</u>.**
   F was steep
   G was dangerous
   H was too steep for a land-based rescue
   J caused another method to be used

3. **In the beginning, Stephen <u>flew high in the sky</u>.**
   A moved upward
   B took to the air
   C soared like an eagle
   D rose above the ground

4. **Stephen had turned the wrong way and <u>caused his glider to drop</u>.**
   F fell toward the ground
   G put his glider into a steep vertical dive
   H went downward with his paraglider
   J was forced down

5. **Miller aimed his fan-powered contraption toward the ring and <u>went down</u>.**
   A landed safely
   B slowly sank
   C began plunging downward
   D moved toward the ring

ANALOGIES As you have seen in previous exercises, analogies show relationships and patterns between words. The relationships can be very different things, not just synonyms and antonyms. For example, *hat* is to *head* as *glove* is to *hand*. The first words (*hat* and *glove*) are meant to cover the second words (*head* and *hand*). For each blank, choose an underlined word from the exercise on this page to correctly complete the analogy. In all cases, you need only one of the words from the underlined phrase to complete the analogy.

1. *Floor* is to *ceiling* as the *earth* is to

   _____ .

2. *Car* is to *bicycle* as *airplane* is to

   _____ .

3. *Harm* is to *endanger* as *save* is to

   _____ .

4. *Rise* is to *up* as *fall* is to

   _____ .

5. *Realistic* is to *unrealistic* as *possible* is to

   _____ .

ORGANIZE THE FACTS There are several different ways to organize your writing. In stories like the ones you just read, the causes (why things happen) and the effects (what happens as a result) are very important. Complete the chart below with the correct cause or effect.

Cause	Effect
made a mistake while flying a paraglider	
	called a helicopter to help
paraglider was out of control	
	championship boxing match was disrupted
Fan Man broke several aviation laws in a foreign country	

ANSWER CAUSE-AND-EFFECT QUESTIONS
Choose the best answer for each question.

1. **What single effect could result from failure to check equipment, flying in bad weather, and making a wrong turn?**

   A crash

   B fun

   C cheer

   D warning

2. **Why did the following events happen?**

   > A boxing match was stopped, a football game was delayed, and public order was disrupted near Buckingham Palace.

   F Bad weather struck.

   G The crowds were unruly.

   H A crazy paraglider landed.

   J A paraglider made a mistake.

MAKE YOUR OWN CAUSE-AND-EFFECT CHART Choose another dangerous sport and fill in the chart.

Cause	Effect

FACT AND OPINION Facts and opinions can sometimes be hard to tell apart. People often represent an opinion as if it were a fact. To tell if something is a fact or an opinion, determine whether what is being said is something that can be proven to be true. If it can, it's a fact. If it states what someone thinks or how someone feels, it's an opinion.

Read this passage about paragliding. Then circle the best answer to each question.

[1] Fly like a bird, soar above beautiful coastal cliffs, and catch a rising hot air balloon up to the cloud base. [2] You can do all this by training with EZParaGliding School. [3] There, you will study with expert pilots. [4] If you are not sure if the sport is right for you, then you should take an introductory tandem flight with Tracy Bailey. [5] She has many hours of tandem flying experience in all conditions from different parts of the world. [6] She has flown in France, Ecuador, Switzerland, New Zealand, and Mexico. [7] Your tandem flights count toward your certification. [8] They are also a great way to learn.

1. **Which sentence from the paragraph states a FACT about Tracy Bailey?**

   A Sentence 2

   B Sentence 3

   C Sentence 4

   D Sentence 5

2. **Which sentence from the paragraph states an OPINION about what it's like to be a paraglider?**

   F Sentence 1

   G Sentence 2

   H Sentence 3

   J Sentence 4

3. **Which sentence from the paragraph most clearly states the author's opinion about tandem flights?**

   A Sentence 5

   B Sentence 6

   C Sentence 7

   D Sentence 8

JUDGE THE EVIDENCE Think back to the stories you have read. Review the paragraph about paragliding in the column on the left. Then choose the best answer.

1. **Which of the following statements is TRUE?**

   A Paragliding does not require special skills.

   B Most people who take up this sport die early.

   C Paragliding can be very dangerous.

   D Paragliding teachers must fly in different parts of the world.

2. **Which of the following statements is FALSE?**

   F Paragliding is safest when you are comfortable with your equipment.

   G There are schools that specialize in paragliding.

   H You can become an expert pilot after taking one flight.

   J You can begin learning the sport by flying in tandem with an expert.

YOUR OPINION Write a brief paragraph expressing your opinion about a dangerous sport. Support your opinions with evidence from the stories you have read.

_____

_____

_____

_____

IN THE WRONG PLACE AT THE WRONG TIME

A Mother's Nightmare

It had been a long and exhausting day for Marcella Anderson. Marcella was traveling alone with her two daughters, 16-month-old Jasmine and 3-year-old Alesia. They had been to visit relatives in St. Louis, Missouri. Now, on Christmas Eve, they were on their way home to Milwaukee, Wisconsin. By the time they reached Chicago, it was already 9:30 P.M. "I was stressed out," Marcella admitted.

Having flown to Chicago, they now planned to take a bus the rest of the way home. As they waited at the Greyhound bus station, Marcella had her hands full. Both girls were getting tired and cranky. Marcella was trying her best to quiet them when a friendly-looking woman approached. She said her name was Christina. When she discovered that Marcella and the girls were going to Milwaukee, she seemed pleasantly surprised. She said she was going that way herself. She offered to give Marcella and the girls a ride.

Gratefully, Marcella accepted the offer. "It was bad judgment," Marcella later acknowledged, "but I was raised to be trusting." Since she no longer needed her bus ticket, she walked over to the ticket window to get a refund. She took Alesia with her. But she left Jasmine sitting with Christina. Marcella stood in line with her back turned for only a few moments. But

that was all it took. Christina grabbed little Jasmine and headed for the door.

When Marcella turned around to check on them, she caught a glimpse of Christina hurrying away with Jasmine. Marcella cried out for help. One man ran after them, but it was too late. Christina and Jasmine had disappeared.

Marcella was stricken with fear and remorse. She did her best to describe Christina to the police. She remembered that the woman had a tattoo on the left side of her neck. It was a word or a name, Marcella said. Marcella also gave the police a picture of Jasmine. Soon the little girl's face was being shown on TV stations across the country.

By the day after Christmas, the police had gotten some tips, but no solid leads. Marcella was desperate. She went to a news conference and spoke to reporters about Jasmine. "All I can think about is her and her little face and not knowing where she's at or who she's with," she said. She also sent out a message to Christina. "I just really wish you would have a heart and a mind to bring her home where she belongs."

No one knew it, but while Marcella was talking to reporters, Jasmine was safe and sound in Illinois. Christina, whose real name was Sheila Matthews, had not harmed the little girl. But she was now pretending that Jasmine was hers.

Sheila wanted a little girl because of a lie she had told her boyfriend. The boyfriend, DeWallis Harris, had been in prison for robbery. While he was serving time, Sheila told him she had given birth to his baby. Now that he was being released from prison, he wanted to see his daughter. So Sheila had to find a toddler she could claim as her own.

After kidnapping Jasmine, Sheila went to the home of Harris' mother, Patricia. She and Jasmine spent the Christmas holiday there with Patricia and DeWallis. But Patricia grew suspicious. She wondered why Sheila didn't know the size of Jasmine's clothes. While Patricia pondered what to do, Sheila and DeWallis took Jasmine to West Virginia to visit relatives there.

On December 27, two of DeWallis' West Virginia relatives saw Jasmine's picture on TV. They thought she looked a lot like Sheila's baby. They called the police. At the same time, Patricia Harris also finally called the police. Authorities responded quickly. Later that day, they moved in. They arrested Sheila and rescued Jasmine.

Marcella jumped on a plane and flew to West Virginia to claim her daughter. Jasmine was asleep when she arrived. "It was the most wonderful feeling in the world," Marcella told reporters. "I was the first person she saw when she woke up and will be the last person she'll see when she goes to sleep."

Marcella Anderson also said that she had learned a tough lesson. She would never again trust a stranger. "No matter what, you have to try to deal with everything on your own," she said.

Mostly, though, Marcella was just happy to be with Jasmine. "I'm just overwhelmed with joy that I got my baby back," she said. Marcella said she knew exactly what she wanted to do first. "We're going to go home [to Milwaukee] as soon as possible and have our own Christmas."

If you have been timed while reading this article, enter your reading time below. Then turn to the Words-per-Minute Table on page 120 and look up your reading speed (words per minute). Enter your reading speed on the graph on page 121.

Reading Time: Selection 1

_____ : _____
MINUTES   SECONDS

UNDERSTANDING IDEAS Circle the letter of the best answer.

1. **When did Marcella leave Jasmine alone with Christina?**

   A when she got to Milwaukee

   B when she was buying her bus ticket

   C when she took Alesia to the rest room

   D when she got a refund on her bus ticket

2. **To what does Marcella attribute her poor judgment that day?**

   F her upbringing

   G her desire to avoid a bus ride

   H having met Christina before

   J her desire to save money

3. **Which of the following statements is FALSE?**

   A Christina was pretending that Jasmine was hers.

   B Christina's boyfriend told her to kidnap Jasmine.

   C Christina took Jasmine to West Virginia for Christmas.

   D Christina was in Illinois with Jasmine.

4. **What did Christina's actions reveal about her character?**

   F She was a liar.

   G She had a good sense of humor.

   H She meant to hurt Jasmine and her family.

   J She was a kind, compassionate person.

SUMMARIZE For each blank, choose the word that best completes the meaning of the paragraph.

| reporters | regret |
| approached | recognized |

Marcella Anderson and her two daughters were waiting at a bus station in Chicago, when a woman named Christina _____ them and offered to drive them home. Marcella accepted but lived to _____ that decision. Christina ran off with Jasmine, her 16-month-old. Marcella spoke to _____, pleading for the return of her daughter. Fortunately, people _____ Jasmine from the picture that had been on TV and called the police.

IF YOU WERE THERE Imagine that you are an old friend of Sheila's and you think she may have kidnapped a baby. Write a brief paragraph explaining what you would do. Be sure to include examples from the story to support your response.

Shocking Shootout

"These guys were ready for war," said Bob McKibben, a storeowner in the North Hollywood section of Los Angeles. "They had black masks over their faces and full black gear, with belts and ammo around their waists."

"These were organized, brutal killers with no respect for human life," said Tim McBride, a spokesman for the Los Angeles Police Department.

McKibben and McBride were talking about two men who walked into a Bank of America branch on February 28, 1997. They were wearing flak jackets and bulletproof pants. They carried AK-47 assault rifles.

They had come to rob the bank. They expected to get about $750,000. That was the amount they had gotten in each of two previous robberies at Bank of America branches. By now, however, bank officials had made some changes. They had started to keep less money in each branch. The North Hollywood bank held only $304,000.

When the robbers, Larry Phillips and Emil Matasareanu, saw that they weren't getting nearly as much money as they had hoped, they became enraged. After telling everyone to lie flat on the floor, they demanded more money from a bank officer. When he told them there was no more, they began to beat him. They also struck a customer in the head with a rifle butt because he failed to keep his baby quiet.

But now, because of the beatings, the robbers' timing was off. They had stayed in the bank longer than they had planned. This gave the police time to respond to a silent alarm that someone in the bank had set off. When the robbers glanced at their watches, they realized their mistake. They rushed out of the bank firing their AK-47s in all directions. At first, the police didn't return fire. They waited until the people running away had a chance to dive for cover. Only then did they begin shooting.

Armando Jimenez was about to go into the bank to cash a check when the robbers came out. He saw them point their guns back into the bank and fire. Then he saw them turn and start firing toward the street. "I just ran," said Jimenez, who found refuge in a neighborhood drugstore. Other people hid behind anything they could find. Tracy Fisher didn't have time to hide. She was simply in the wrong place at the wrong time. As she headed for the bank's ATM, both she and her dog were shot and wounded.

Bullets were flying everywhere. "It was like the OK Corral," said passer-by Nancy Swanson.

Demond Trotter was driving by the bank at the time. Suddenly he realized he was in the crossfire. "You could feel the bullets in the air," he said. "You could hear the pop, pop, pop."

The police did their best, but the two robbers had a big advantage. The police bullets were not designed to penetrate metal. They were not built to go through walls or cars. That was supposed to reduce the risk of hitting innocent bystanders. The police bullets couldn't go through the robbers' bulletproof clothes, either. But Philips and Matasareanu had high-powered AK-47s. Their bullets could penetrate almost anything.

Police Officer Dennis Zine told what it was like trying to shoot one of the robbers. "Our bullets bounced off him just like Superman," Zine said. "He just kept on firing back."

Eventually, Matasareanu made his way to a getaway car. Philips stayed in the parking lot, shooting round after round at police. Clearly the police needed stronger weapons. Some officers raced to a local gun store. They returned with semiautomatics, shotguns, and rifles.

The gun battle lasted more than half an hour. Over two hundred police officers took part. Bullets shattered car windshields and bounced off the pavement. TV cameras caught the whole thing as TV helicopters buzzed overhead. At last, Philips turned his gun on himself and committed suicide. Matasareanu tried to flee in the getaway car. He drove two blocks before the police shot out his tires. He then tried to steal a pickup truck. But the driver ran off with the truck keys. Matasareanu ran behind the getaway car and continued to fire his weapon.

At last, police were able to pepper Matasareanu with bullets. He slumped to the ground. Before an ambulance could get him to the hospital, he bled to death. Remarkably, no one else died. Still, eleven police officers and five civilians were wounded. David Hepburn, the president of the police union, said, "I don't ever remember having this many officers wounded in one incident."

The people in the neighborhood had high praise for the police. Noubar Torossian, whose house was riddled by bullets, later said, "The policemen saved our lives, and I want to say, 'Thank you, thank you, a million times, thank you.'"

If you have been timed while reading this article, enter your reading time below. Then turn to the Words-per-Minute Table on page 120 and look up your reading speed (words per minute). Enter your reading speed on the graph on page 121.

Reading Time: Selection 2

_____ : _____
MINUTES   SECONDS

UNDERSTANDING IDEAS Circle the letter of the best answer.

1. **What does the clothing of the robbers suggest about them?**

   A They were hoping to get a lot of money.

   B They had not planned the robbery in advance.

   C They did not want anyone to remember how they looked.

   D They were experienced robbers who did not want to get caught.

2. **What outraged the robbers at the Bank of America that day in Los Angeles?**

   F finding less money than they expected

   G the length of time it took to rob the bank

   H beating a bank officer who wouldn't talk

   J the silent alarm system that alerted the police

3. **Initially, the police did not return fire because**

   A they did not have ample firepower

   B the robbers had injured a bank customer

   C they couldn't see the robbers well enough to get a clear shot

   D they wanted to give people a chance to take cover

4. **Which statement would Emil Matasareanu most likely make?**

   F "I never meant to hurt anyone."

   G "I want to avenge the death of my partner."

   H "I will die before I will let myself be arrested."

   J "I only want the money; I don't want to commit murder."

SUMMARIZE For each blank, choose the word that best completes the meaning of the paragraph.

masked	exchanged	
		bulletproof
alarm	terrorized	

On February 28, 1997, two _____ men entered a Bank of America in Los Angeles. The men took money and _____ the bank customers. Someone in the bank managed to set off a silent _____, and police arrived, surprising the robbers. The police and the robbers _____ fire for over half an hour. Because the robbers were wearing _____ clothing, they were almost impossible to stop.

IF YOU WERE THERE Write a brief paragraph explaining what you would have done if you were in the bank the day of the robery. Be sure to include examples from the story to support your response.

_____

_____

_____

_____

_____

_____

USE CONTEXT CLUES When you read, you may find a word whose meaning is unfamiliar to you. When that happens, you can look up the word's meaning in the dictionary. You can also find out what the word means by looking for context clues. These are words or sentences that come before or after the word. Context clues can be synonyms or antonyms of the unfamiliar word. They may also be an example or definition of the unfamiliar word.

Read each excerpt from the stories you just read. Circle the letter with the best meaning of the underlined word.

1. **Marcella had her hands full. Both girls were getting tired and cranky.**
   A grouchy
   B scared
   C silly
   D unsure

2. **Christina and Jasmine had disappeared. Marcella was stricken with fear and remorse.**
   F confused
   G fatigued
   H concerned
   J overcome

3. **By the day after Christmas, the police had gotten some tips but no solid leads.**
   A arrests
   B clues
   C convictions
   D suspects

4. **But Patricia grew suspicious. She wondered why Sheila didn't know the size of Jasmine's clothes. While Patricia pondered what to do, Sheila and DeWallis took Jasmine to West Virginia to visit some relatives there.**
   F argued
   G suspected
   H thought hard about
   J watched out

5. **The police bullets were not designed to penetrate metal. They were not built to go through walls or cars.**
   A pierce
   B touch
   C repel
   D attract

PUT WORDS INTO CONTEXT Complete the paragraph using the underlined words from the exercise on this page.

Jasmine Anderson had been at the bus station with her mother and sister. Her mother was trying to manage two _____ children when a helpful woman named Christina offered to drive them to Milwaukee. When Marcella left Jasmine with Christina for just a moment, Christina took off with Jasmine. There were no good _____ about where little Jasmine was. Her mother, Marcella, was _____ with fear at the thought of what might happen to her daughter. Police _____ where she could be. After seeing Jasmine's picture on TV, DeWallis Harris' relatives recognized her and called the police.

SIMILES AND METAPHORS Writers use similes and metaphors to make their writing more vivid. Similes and metaphors are comparisons between words. Similes are easy to spot because they include the words *like* or *as*. Here's an example: *She was poised like a cat ready to pounce.* Here is another simile: *Ira was as cunning as a snake.* Metaphors are a little different because the comparisons do not use the words *like* or *as*. Here's an example of a metaphor: *The nurse was an angel of mercy.* In this metaphor, "nurse" is compared with "angel of mercy."

Read the following sentences. Decide whether the comparison is a simile or metaphor. Write S for simile or M for metaphor in the blank on the left.

_____ **1.** Bullets of fear pierced the bank teller's heart.

_____ **2.** The gun battle was a modern day OK Corral.

_____ **3.** The bank customer was shaking like a leaf.

_____ **4.** Phillips and Matasareanu took over the bank like a storm, waving guns and shouting orders.

_____ **5.** Bullets fell like rain in the streets of Los Angeles.

WHAT'S THE COMPARISON? Read the following sentences. In the space provided, write what two things are being compared.

1. Like savages, the robbers hit the man holding a crying baby.

_____

2. Philips and Matasareanu were warriors ready to kill.

_____

3. The kidnapping was a nightmare for Marcella.

_____

4. The robbers were like Superman; bullets bounced off their chests.

_____

5. "It [the gun battle] was like the OK Corral," said passer-by Nancy Swanson.

_____

PRACTICE SUMMARIZING As you now know, a summary retells the main points of a story. Summaries do not attempt to recount every detail. For example, if you look up a TV guide in the newspaper, there is often a summary of what each show is about. A sentence is usually enough to summarize a half-hour program.

Practice writing one-sentence summaries of these books about kidnapping and bank robbery. Use only one sentence. You decide what the book will be about, based on the title. The first one is done for you.

Book Title and One-sentence Summary
1. *Missing Since Dawn*   <u>Little Isis Brown was taken from her family's</u>   <u>home at day break a year ago and is still missing.</u>
2. *Jon Green, a.k.a. The Kansas City Kidnapper*
3. *Lawyer by Day, Thief by Night*
4. *Sleep, Eat, Steal—A Bank Robber's Life*

SUMMARIZE THE STORIES In the space provided, write a one-paragraph summary of each of the stories. Be sure to include only the main points from each selection.

"A Mother's Nightmare"

"Shocking Shootout"

MAKE INFERENCES Inferences are what the reader learns from what the writer has written. When you make an inference, you consider the evidence you've read and then decide what the message is. Circle the letter of the best answer.

1. **What can the reader infer from the following sentences?**

> It had been a long and exhausting day for Marcella Anderson. Marcella was traveling alone with her two daughters. By the time they reached Chicago, it was already 9:30 P.M. "I was stressed out," Marcella admitted.

   A The children were behaving badly.

   B It is difficult to travel around the holidays.

   C Marcella was feeling tired and overwhelmed.

   D Marcella always exercises bad judgment.

2. **What can the reader infer about Shelia's intentions from the following paragraph?**

> Christina, whose real name was Sheila Matthews, had not harmed the little girl. But she was now pretending that Jasmine was hers.

   F Jasmine was happier in her new home.

   G Jasmine was in better hands with Sheila.

   H Sheila eventually intended to kill Jasmine.

   J Sheila planned to keep Jasmine permanently.

APPLY WHAT YOU KNOW

1. **What do you think the author's main purpose was in the first paragraph of "A Mother's Nightmare"?**

   A to tell the reader Marcella's travel schedule

   B to show Marcella's physical and emotional state

   C to list the names of Marcella's daughters

   D to suggest that Marcella was a bad mother

2. **Read the following sentences. What overall impression is the author trying to give about Sheila?**

> Sheila wanted a little girl because of a lie she had told her boyfriend. While he was in prison, Sheila told him she had given birth to his baby. Now that he was being released from prison, he wanted to see his daughter. So Sheila had to find a toddler she could claim as her own.

   F She was afraid of her boyfriend.

   G She wanted to break up with Harris.

   H She would rather kidnap a baby than tell the truth.

   J She loved kids and wanted a family.

JUDGE THE EVIDENCE Based on what you have read from both stories, are there any similarities between the kidnapper, Sheila Matthews, and the robbers Larry Phillips and Emil Matasareanu? Support your opinions with evidence from the stories you have read.

_____

_____

_____

_____

_____

_____

SELECTION 1

The Hunt for a Killer

Labor Day weekend in the year 2000 wasn't a pleasant experience for Jeff Stevenson. At first he felt as if he was coming down with the flu. He had a fever, achy muscles, and chills. Then his symptoms got worse. Stevenson began coughing and he had trouble breathing. This was not the flu, he realized. It was something more serious. So he went to a hospital in Flagstaff, Arizona, to see what was wrong.

At the hospital, Stevenson suddenly collapsed. His heart stopped beating for eight minutes. It took a team of doctors and nurses to save him. For three weeks Stevenson lay in a coma while a heart-lung machine kept him alive. Nelson Stevenson, Jeff's father, remembered how the hospital staff greeted him when he first came to see Jeff. "When I got there, the nurse asked me if I wanted to speak to the chaplain," said Mr. Stevenson. "The doctors told me he had less than a ten percent chance to live."

In late September, Jeff Stevenson finally opened his eyes. He was going to live, but it would take months of rehabilitation before he could go back to work. What had nearly killed a seemingly healthy 44-year-old man? Actually, Stevenson had suspected the cause before he slipped into the coma. "I read about all the Indian boys who got sick back in 1993," he said. "I was aware of it. When I went to the hospital,

the doctor said I had pneumonia and I said, 'No, I've got something worse.'"

What he had was hantavirus. The story of this strange disease began in May 1993. That's when several healthy young Navajo suddenly became sick and died. Some unknown disease was causing their lungs to fill up with fluid. They were, in effect, drowning. One of the victims was Merrill Bahe. He was just twenty years old and one of the fastest cross-country runners in the state. His doctors couldn't figure out why he got so sick and died so quickly. What made the case even stranger was the fact that Merrill's 21-year-old fiancée, Florena Woody, had died just a few days earlier. In fact, Merrill died on the day of Florena's funeral. Like Merrill, Florena had been perfectly healthy just a few days before her death.

Doctors determined that the victims' lungs had sprung countless leaks. This allowed fluid to seep into the lungs and push out the oxygen. Without oxygen, the heart stopped. "It was really pretty dramatic," said Bruce Tempest, chief of infectious diseases at the Gallup Indian Medical Center. Autopsies showed that Merrill's and Florena's lungs weighed three times what they should have weighed. Their lungs had also turned purple. Doctors had seen lungs like this before. But they had only seen them in heroin addicts or people with advanced heart disease. These two Navajo had normal hearts, and tests proved that neither had used drugs.

Doctors wondered if the Navajo were the only ones who were vulnerable to this new disease. Then an Icelandic woman who lived in New Mexico also died from it. That showed that the disease could strike anyone.

Between May and June of 1993, thirteen people died from this disease. A team of specialists worked frantically to find the culprit. Was it a poison? Was it a virus? Was it some kind of bacterium? The specialists took thousands of blood samples. They collected fleas from pets. They asked countless questions. In less than one month, they found what they were looking for. The villain was the common deer mouse. This mouse carried a virus in its saliva and waste products. When people breathed in dust contaminated by the saliva or waste products, the deadly hantavirus could enter their system.

Once scientists knew what caused hantavirus, they could take some preventive measures. They warned people to keep mice out of homes and outbuildings. But doctors still had no cure for the disease. The best they could do was to diagnose hantavirus quickly and then try to keep the victim's lungs drained of fluid. Unfortunately, an early diagnosis was hard to make. The early symptoms of the disease were like those of the flu or

other milder illnesses. That was why Jeff Stevenson's doctors misdiagnosed his ailment at first. Since 1993, there have been close to 300 reported cases of hantavirus. Nearly 40 percent of these victims have died.

Hantavirus almost killed Dan Bradshaw of Colorado. One day in 1996, Bradshaw used a broom to sweep out a mouse-infested building. Then he slept in the building. Soon afterwards, Bradshaw developed a bad cough. He began to have trouble breathing, and he experienced frequent blackouts. It took visits to four doctors before he got the correct diagnosis.

Luckily, hantavirus didn't kill Bradshaw. Still, it left him only a shell of the athlete he once was. He had been a bike racer and a marathon runner. The disease badly damaged his lungs. Bradshaw couldn't bike or run the way he once had. Other people, he hoped, wouldn't make the mistake he made. "I should have recognized that [cleaning the building] was a dangerous situation and come back with the proper equipment to clean it up," he said. "People don't need to get this disease."

If you have been timed while reading this article, enter your reading time below. Then turn to the Words-per-Minute Table on page 120 and look up your reading speed (words per minute). Enter your reading speed on the graph on page 121.

Reading Time: Selection 1

_____ : _____
MINUTES   SECONDS

UNDERSTANDING IDEAS Circle the letter of the best answer.

1. **Why did Jeff Stevenson go to the hospital?**

   A He was having blackouts.

   B He realized his condition was more serious than the flu.

   C He had cleaned a dirty building.

   D He did not have a pleasant Labor Day weekend.

2. **What clue did Stevenson have about the cause of his illness?**

   F He read about Navajo boys getting sick.

   G The doctor told him he had pneumonia.

   H He had collapsed and slipped into a coma.

   J He was drowning because of the fluid in his lungs.

3. **Which of the following statements is FALSE about hantavirus?**

   A It makes the lungs fill with fluid.

   B It can kill before it is even diagnosed.

   C It is carried by a common deer mouse.

   D Only the Navajo can suffer from the disease.

4. **Based on Dan Bradshaw's experience, which of the following will he most likely avoid?**

   F biking leisurely in a park

   G walking or running for exercise

   H cleaning a mouse-infested building

   J visiting doctors when he has trouble breathing

SUMMARIZE For each blank, choose the word that best completes the meaning of the paragraph.

heart	flu	worse
cure	hantavirus	coma

Jeff Stevenson thought he only had the

_____. But after his symptoms

got dramatically _____, he knew

it was something much more serious. When he got to

the hospital, his _____ stopped

beating for eight minutes. He spent three weeks in a

_____. Jeff had contracted

_____, a virus that causes

the lungs to fill with fluid. There is still no

_____, but the disease is easier

to prevent if the cause is known.

IF YOU WERE THERE Write a brief paragraph explaining what you would do if you thought you might have the hantavirus. Be sure to include examples from the story in your response.

_____

_____

_____

_____

_____

How Now Mad Cow

"First comes the pain and crying," reported the Akron Beacon Journal on June 3, 2001. "Then the hallucinations and screaming. As the fatal disease progresses, the victim loses all motion and all reason. The brain becomes riddled with holes. When death comes, it is a blessing."

Welcome to the world of mad cow disease. As its name suggests, this disease first showed up in cattle. In 1986, English farmers noticed that some of their cows were acting strangely. The animals began to drool uncontrollably. Their legs grew wobbly. Some made threatening gestures at other cattle. These cows grew sicker and sicker. Finally they died.

The problem came from the cattle's diet. British farmers had been using feed that included brain and spinal tissue from dead sheep. They did this to give their cattle more protein. But now it was giving the animals something else—a death sentence.

Farmers switched to different feed, but in many cases it was too late. Thousands of cows had already been infected. The disease lay dormant in some cows for up to five years. But sooner or later, they grew sick and died. By 1993, mad cow disease was killing a thousand cows a week in England.

At that point, the problem had not affected humans. But people were worried. If humans ate beef from sick cows, would the people get sick, too? For years, the British government insisted they would not. In 1990, British Agricultural Secretary John Gummer went on TV. He wanted to show how safe it was to eat British beef. In living color he wolfed down a hamburger. His four-year-old daughter, Cordelia, did the same thing. In 1995, Prime Minister John Major also tried to calm people's fears. "There is currently no scientific evidence that [mad cow disease] can be transmitted to humans," he said.

But many people were not convinced. A few individuals were coming down with a new disease that seemed similar to mad cow disease. Doctors called it "variant Creutzfeldt-Jacob disease," or "vCJD." Many people thought it was the human version of mad cow disease. Nora Greenhalgh was one of them. Greenhalgh lost her 38-year-old daughter to vCJD. In her grief and anger, she wrote a letter to Major. He answered by repeating that there was no proven link between mad cow disease and the human disease. "I didn't believe him then, and I don't believe him now," said Greenhalgh.

Muriel Jones had a similar reaction. She lost her daughter, Christine Hay, to vCJD. "My heart goes out to any family that has to go through what we went through," she said. "The government is trying to sweep the issue under the carpet."

At last, in March of 1996, scientists found a link between mad cow disease and vCJD. The next day France banned the importation of all British beef. Over the next three days, 23 more countries did the same thing. In response, Britain decided to slaughter four million of its cows.

But diseased animal feed was still being sold. Some of this contaminated feed made its way to European farmers. By 2000, mad cow disease began to show up in France, Germany, and Spain. In 1996, only nine British people died from vCJD. By 2001, 91 people had died. Almost all were British, but a few came from other European countries.

Many people decided to change *what* they ate. Beef dishes disappeared from school lunches and restaurant menus. Thousands gave up meat altogether and became vegetarians. Europeans who still wanted some kind of meat switched to chicken or pork. More exotic meats became popular. People ate ostrich and kangaroo meat. Some switched to crocodile meat. Germans began stuffing their sausages with meat from horses. One newspaper even printed a recipe for nutria. Some red wine and garlic, it reported, turned this rodent into a mouthwatering delight.

Meanwhile, cattle farmers saw their way of life being destroyed. One of these farmers was Denis Veys of Belgium. His family had raised cattle for generations. In 2000, one of his cows came down with mad cow disease. The government seized his entire herd of 131 cattle and destroyed them all. "This is a criminal thing," said Veys, who wondered how he would support his family.

Butchers weren't too happy either. With Europeans eating less beef, their business suffered. Some of them put signs in their windows stating that they only sold beef from South America. Still, their profits plummeted. "People talk a lot about mad cow," said butcher Gerard Esnault of France, "But I think it's the people who have gone a little bit mad."

No one knows what will happen with mad cow disease over the next ten or twenty years. But one thing is certain. Everyone now agrees that it's a serious problem. Even people like Paris chef Alain Passard are concerned. Passard works at L'Arpege restaurant. People pay more than $300 to eat the food he prepares. Passard reacted to the crisis by getting rid of twelve of his famous meat dishes. He announced that he would now tantalize his customers with "the simple onion, the simple carrot, even a turnip." Imagine paying $300 for a plate of carrots. *Bon appetite!*

If you have been timed while reading this article, enter your reading time below. Then turn to the Words-per-Minute Table on page 120 and look up your reading speed (words per minute). Enter your reading speed on the graph on page 121.

Reading Time: Selection 2

_____ : _____
MINUTES   SECONDS

UNDERSTANDING IDEAS Circle the letter of the best answer.

1. **Which of the following is NOT a symptom of mad cow disease?**

    A loss of motion and reason

    B need for more protein in food

    C hallucinations and screaming

    D brain becomes riddled with holes

2. **Probably the biggest concern about mad cow disease was**

    F that the cause would not be found

    G whether it was transferable to humans

    H that it would spread outside Britain

    J what would happen to the beef industry

3. **What conclusion can the reader draw from the following comment by Muriel Jones?**

    > "The government is trying to sweep the issue under the carpet."

    A She feels that all the cattle in Britain should be slaughtered.

    B She thinks that the government is spending too much money researching the disease.

    C She believes that the government is hiding the fact that humans can get the disease.

    D She is firm in her belief that there is no link between mad cow disease and vCJD.

4. **Based on people's reactions to mad cow disease in Europe, what would most likely happen if the disease were found in the United States?**

    F Americans would eat less beef.

    G American scientists would find a cure.

    H American restaurants would serve more meat.

    J All Americans would become vegetarians.

SUMMARIZE For each blank, choose the word that best completes the meaning of the paragraph.

appearance	dying	link
discovered	cattle	scientific

The first _____ of mad cow disease in England was in 1986. Farmers noticed that many of their cows were getting sick and _____. By the time the cause of mad cow disease was _____, it was too late. Thousands of _____ had been infected. People began to think that humans could get mad cow disease, although there was no _____ proof. Later it was discovered that there was a _____ between the two.

IF YOU WERE THERE Write a brief paragraph explaining what you would do if some cows in your country were found to have mad cow disease. Be sure to include examples from the story to support your response.

_____

_____

_____

_____

_____

_____

USE CONTEXT CLUES When you read, you may find a word whose meaning is unfamiliar to you. When that happens, you can look up the word's meaning in the dictionary. You can also find out what the word means by looking for context clues. These are words or sentences that come before or after the word. Context clues can be synonyms or antonyms of the unfamiliar word. They may also be an example or definition of the unfamiliar word.

Read each excerpt from the stories you just read. Circle the letter with the best meaning of the underlined word.

1. **In late September, Jeff Stevenson finally opened his eyes. He was going to live, but it would take months of <u>rehabilitation</u> before he could go back to work.**

   A doctor's visits

   B prescriptions

   C therapy that helps recovery

   D operations

2. **<u>Autopsies</u> showed that Merrill's and Florena's lungs weighed three times what they should have weighed. Their lungs had also turned purple.**

   F physical therapies

   G examinations after death

   H educated guesses

   J X-rays

3. **Between May and June of 1993, thirteen people died from this disease. A team of specialists worked frantically to find the <u>culprit</u>. Was it a poison? Was it a virus?**

   A guilty party, reason

   B infected person

   C cure

   D antidote

4. **Farmers switched to different feed, but in many cases it was too late. Thousands of cows had already been infected. The disease lay <u>dormant</u> in some cows for up to five years. But sooner or later, they grew sick and died.**

   F under the skin

   G multiplying

   H in the fields

   J inactive

5. **Butchers weren't too happy either. With Europeans eating less beef, their business suffered. Some of them put signs in their windows stating that they only sold beef from South America. Still, their profits <u>plummeted</u>.**

   A plunged downward

   B rose quickly

   C dropped slowly

   D skyrocketed

PUT WORDS INTO CONTEXT Complete the paragraph using the underlined words from the exercise on this page.

Merrill Bahe and his fiancée, Florena Woody, died within a few days of each other, but doctors could not determine the _____. After _____ were performed on both Merrill and Florena, doctors found that their lungs were full of fluid and weighed nearly three times the normal weight. Jeff Stevenson's story has a happier ending. He too became terribly ill. He did not die, but had to endure months of _____ before he could return to work.

SUFFIXES A suffix is one or more letters added to the end of a word to change its meaning. For example, the suffix –*dom* means "a state of being." So when you add the suffix –*dom* to the word *free*, you get *freedom*, which means "the state of being free."

Use a dictionary to find the meaning of each suffix below. Match the suffix with its meaning on the right. Examples for each definition are included in italics. Write the letter of the correct definition on the line.

_____ **1.** -able   **A** process or action: *motivation*

_____ **2.** -ous   **B** to cause, become: *dramatize*

_____ **3.** -ize   **C** state or condition: *dependence*

_____ **4.** -tion   **D** capable, worthy of: *debatable*

_____ **5.** -ence   **E** one who performs a specfic action: *swimmer*

_____ **6.** -al   **F** without: *fruitless*

_____ **7.** -less   **G** full of: *joyous*

_____ **8.** -er   **H** characterized by: *ornamental*

WRITE DEFINITIONS In the exercise below, underline the suffix, and write the meaning of the word on the line provided.

1. completion

    definition: _____

2. blameless

    definition: _____

3. dangerous

    definition: _____

4. realize

    definition: _____

5. criminal

    definition: _____

6. difference

    definition: _____

7. changeable

    definition: _____

8. farmer

    definition: _____

ORGANIZE IDEAS The main ideas in a story are the main topics that are discussed. The specific details are the facts that clarify or support the main ideas. Fill in the chart by using the items listed at the right. If the bulleted item is a main idea from the story, write it in the row marked "Main Idea." If the item is a detail that supports the main idea, write it in a row marked "Detail."

"The Hunt for a Killer"
Main Idea:
Detail:
Detail:
Detail:
Detail:

"How Now Mad Cow"
Main Idea:
Detail:
Detail:
Detail:
Detail:

- Dan Bradshaw swept out a mouse-infested building.

- Britain decided to slaughter four million cows.

- Jeff Stevenson was in a coma for three weeks.

- Mad cow disease first showed up in cattle and was later linked to the vCJD virus in humans.

- The disease comes from feed made with the brain and spinal tissue of sheep.

- In May of 1993, several young Navajo suddenly became ill and died.

- Muriel Jones lost her daughter to vCJD.

- Hantavirus can kill humans or make them very sick.

- Cattle farmers watched their way of life destroyed.

- Between May and June of 1993, thirteen people died from this disease.

SUPPORT THE MAIN IDEA Write a paragraph about sudden outbreaks of disease. State the main idea in the first sentence. Then use details from both stories to support your main idea.

_____

_____

_____

_____

_____

VERIFYING EVIDENCE Because a lot of misinformation gets printed, you must verify the accuracy of everything you read. The way to do that is to weigh the evidence presented and decide whether it is trustworthy. Sometimes part of an article may present the correct facts about something, and part of the same article may mislead you. You have to decide whether to believe all or only parts of the information you've read.

Read the following sentences taken from "How Now Mad Cow." Choose the best answer for each question.

[1] "I didn't believe him [Prime Minister John Major] then, and I don't believe him now," said Greenhalgh. [2] Muriel Jones had a similar reaction. [3] She lost her daughter, Christine Hay, to vCJD. [4] "My heart goes out to any family that has to go through what we went through," she said. [5] "The government is trying to sweep the issue under the carpet."

1. **What evidence would best support Jones' claim about the government?**

    A hearing the same opinion from several people

    B reading a news article about mad cow disease

    C the testimony of a highly placed government worker

    D reading an editorial about the government's handling of the disease

2. **Which sentence in the paragraph would be most difficult to verify?**

    F Sentence 2

    G Sentence 3

    H Sentence 4

    J Sentence 5

JUDGE THE EVIDENCE To persuade the reader, the author often provides evidence. It is up to the reader to judge if the evidence presented is believable or not.

1. **Which of the following provides the MOST convincing evidence that the world was worried about contracting vCJD from diseased cattle?**

    A a documentary about world economics and health

    B British Agricultural Secretary John Gummer's learned opinion

    C the publication of a report linking mad cow disease to vCJD virus in humans

    D France and 23 other countries banned the importation of British beef.

2. **Which statement provides the MOST convincing evidence that Europeans changed the way they lived their daily lives because of mad cow disease?**

    F Some restaurants stopped serving beef.

    G Thousands of people became vegetarians.

    H Butchers advertised that they sold only South American beef.

    J all of the above

PERSUADE WITH EVIDENCE Write two sentences persuading your reader that mad cow disease is a serious national and international problem. Be sure to include examples from the story to support your answer.

_____

_____

_____

_____

Words-per-Minute Table

If you were timed while reading, find your reading time in the column on the left. Find the unit and number of the story across the top of the chart. Follow the time row across to its intersection with the column of the story. This is your reading speed. Go to the next page to plot your progress.

Unit Selection Time	1-1	1-2	2-1	2-2	3-1	3-2	4-1	4-2	5-1	5-2	6-1	6-2	7-1	7-2	8-1	8-2	9-1	9-2	10-1	10-2
1:20	892	938	805	836	874	785	754	877	788	833	904	806	857	827	779	776	770	802	871	876
1:40	669	704	604	627	656	589	566	658	591	625	678	605	643	620	584	582	578	602	653	657
2:00	535	563	483	501	524	471	452	526	473	500	542	484	514	496	467	466	462	481	522	525
2:20	446	469	403	418	437	393	377	439	394	417	452	403	429	414	390	388	385	401	436	438
2:40	382	402	345	358	375	336	323	376	338	357	387	345	367	354	334	333	330	344	373	375
3:00	334	352	302	313	328	294	283	329	295	312	339	302	321	310	292	291	289	301	327	328
3:20	297	313	268	279	291	262	251	292	263	278	301	269	286	276	260	259	257	267	290	292
3:40	268	281	242	251	262	236	226	263	236	250	271	242	257	248	234	233	231	241	261	263
4:00	243	256	220	228	238	214	206	239	215	227	247	220	234	226	212	212	210	219	238	239
4:20	223	235	201	209	219	196	189	219	197	208	226	202	214	207	195	194	193	201	218	219
4:40	206	216	186	193	202	181	174	202	182	192	209	186	198	191	180	179	178	185	201	202
5:00	191	201	172	179	187	168	162	188	169	178	194	173	184	177	167	166	165	172	187	188
5:20	178	188	161	167	175	157	151	175	158	167	181	161	171	165	156	155	154	160	174	175
5:40	167	176	151	157	164	147	141	164	148	156	170	151	161	155	146	146	144	150	163	164
6:00	157	166	142	148	154	139	133	155	139	147	160	142	151	146	137	137	136	142	154	155
6:20	149	156	134	139	146	131	126	146	131	139	151	134	143	138	130	129	128	134	145	146
6:40	141	148	127	132	138	124	119	138	124	132	143	127	135	131	123	123	122	127	138	138
7:00	134	141	121	125	131	118	113	132	118	125	136	121	129	124	117	116	115	120	131	131
7:20	127	134	115	119	125	112	108	125	113	119	129	115	122	118	111	111	110	115	124	125
7:40	122	128	110	114	119	107	103	120	107	114	123	110	117	113	106	106	105	109	119	119
8:00	116	122	105	109	114	102	98	114	103	109	118	105	112	108	102	101	100	105	114	114
8:20	112	117	101	105	109	98	94	110	99	104	113	101	107	103	97	97	96	100	109	110
8:40	107	113	97	100	105	94	90	105	95	100	108	97	103	99	93	93	92	96	105	105
9:00	103	108	93	96	101	91	87	101	91	96	104	93	99	95	90	90	89	93	100	101
9:20	99	104	89	93	97	87	84	97	88	93	100	90	95	92	87	86	86	89	97	97
9:40	96	101	86	90	94	84	81	94	84	89	97	86	92	89	83	83	83	86	93	94
10:00	92	97	83	86	90	81	78	91	82	86	94	83	89	86	81	80	80	83	90	91
10:20	89	94	81	84	87	79	75	88	79	83	90	81	86	83	78	78	77	80	87	88
10:40	86	91	78	81	85	76	73	85	76	81	87	78	83	80	75	75	75	78	84	85
11:00	84	88	75	78	82	74	71	82	74	78	85	76	80	78	73	73	72	75	82	82
11:20	81	85	73	76	79	71	69	80	72	76	82	73	78	75	71	71	70	73	79	80
11:40	79	83	71	74	77	69	67	75	70	74	80	71	76	73	69	68	68	71	77	77
12:00	76	80	69	72	75	67	65	73	68	71	77	69	73	71	67	67	66	69	75	75
12:20	74	78	67	70	73	65	63	71	66	69	75	67	71	69	65	65	64	67	73	73
12:40	72	76	65	68	71	64	61	69	64	68	73	65	69	67	63	63	62	65	71	71
13:00	70	74	64	66	69	62	60	67	62	66	71	64	68	65	61	61	61	63	69	69
13:20	69	72	62	64	67	60	58	65	61	64	70	62	66	63	60	60	59	62	67	67
13:40	67	70	60	63	66	59	57	64	59	61	68	60	64	61	58	58	58	60	65	66
14:00	65	69	59	61	64	57	55	61	58	60	66	59	63	60	57	57	56	59	64	64
14:20	64	67	58	60	62	56	54	60	56	58	65	58	61	58	56	55	55	57	62	63
14:40	62	65	56	58	61	55	53	58	55	57	63	56	60	56	54	54	54	56	61	61
15:00	59	63	54	56	58	52	50	58	53	56	60	54	57	55	52	52	51	53	58	58

Plotting Your Progress: Reading Speed

Enter your words-per-minute rate in the box above the appropriate lesson. Then place a small X on the line directly above the number of the lesson, across from the number of words per minute you read. Graph your progress by drawing a line to connect the X's.

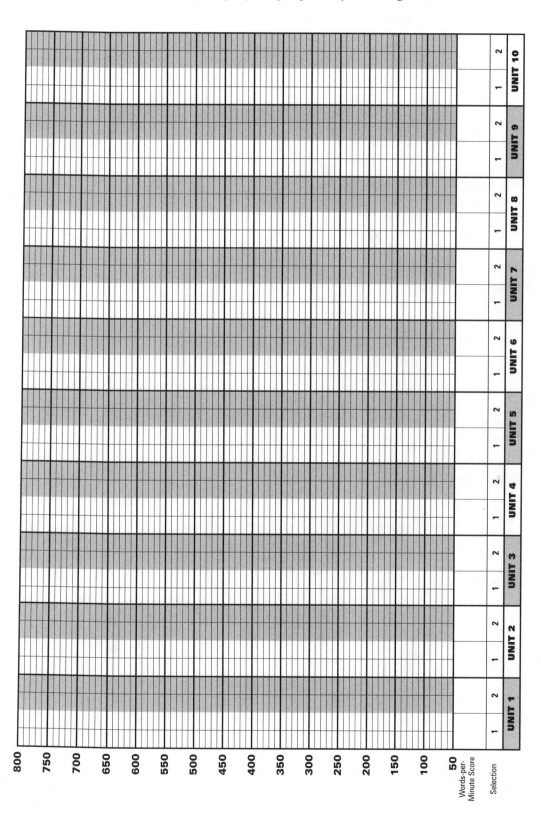

Photo Credits